THE MAKING OF
CHRISTIAN DOCTRINE

THE MAKING
OF CHRISTIAN
DOCTRINE

A STUDY IN THE PRINCIPLES OF
EARLY DOCTRINAL DEVELOPMENT

BY

MAURICE WILES

Regius Professor of Divinity,
University of Oxford

CAMBRIDGE UNIVERSITY PRESS

CAMBRIDGE

LONDON · NEW YORK · MELBOURNE

Published by the Syndics of the Cambridge University Press
The Pitt Building, Trumpington Street, Cambridge CB2 1RP
Bentley House, 200 Euston Road, London NW1 2DB
32 East 57th Street, New York, NY 10022, USA
296 Beaconsfield Parade, Middle Park, Melbourne 3206, Australia

Library of Congress catalogue card number: 67-10081

ISBN 0 521 06803 7 hard covers
ISBN 0 521 09962 5 paperback

First published 1967
First paperback edition 1975
Reprinted 1978

First printed in Great Britain
at the University Press, Cambridge
Reprinted in Great Britain by Lewis Reprints
London and Tonbridge

CONTENTS

ABBREVIATIONS

The following standard abbreviations have been used:

C.Q.R.	*Church Quarterly Review*
E.T.	English translation
J.E.H.	*Journal of Ecclesiastical History*
J.T.S.	*Journal of Theological Studies*
P.G.	*Patrologia Graeca, Cursus Completus*, ed. J.-P. Migne
P.L.	*Patrologia Latina, Cursus Completus*, ed. J.-P. Migne
R.H.E.	*Revue d'Histoire Ecclésiastique*
R.S.R.	*Recherches de Science Religieuse*

The following abbreviations for patristic references have been used in the notes:

Ap. Const.	*Apostolic Constitutions*
Athanasius, *Or. Con. Ar.*	*Orationes Contra Arianos*
De. Inc.	*De Incarnatione*
Ep(p). ad Ser.	*Epistola(e) ad Serapionem*
pseudo-Athanasius, *Con. Apoll.*	*De Incarnatione contra Apollinarem*
Basil, *Adv. Eun.*	*Adversus Eunomium*
De Spir. San.	*De Spiritu Sancto*
Ep(p).	*Epistle(s)*
Chrysostom, *Hom. in Joh.*	*Homiliae in Johannem*
Clement of Alexandria, *Paid.*	*Paidagogos*
Strom.	*Stromateis*

ABBREVIATIONS

Cyprian, *De Un. Cath. Eccl.*	*De Unitate Catholicae Ecclesiae*
Cyril of Jerusalem, *Cat.*	*Catecheses*
Eusebius, *H.E.*	*Historia Ecclesiastica*
Gregory of Nazianzus, *Or.*	*Orationes*
Gregory of Nyssa, *Con. Eun.*	*Contra Eunomium*
Or. Cat.	*Oratio Catechetica Magna*
Hermas, *M.*	*'Shepherd' of Hermas, Mandates*
Hippolytus, *Haer.*	*Refutatio Omnium Haeresium*
Irenaeus, *Adv. Haer.*	*Adversus Haereses*
Justin Martyr, *Apol.*	*Apologia*
Dial.	*Dialogos cum Tryphone*
Origen, *Con. Cel.*	*Contra Celsum*
Comm. Jn.	*Commentarium in Johannem*
Matt. Comm. Ser.	*Commentariorum in Matthaeum Series*
De Or.	*De Oratione*
De Princ.	*De Principiis*
Philostorgius, *H.E.*	*Historia Ecclesiastica*
Tertullian, *Adv. Jud.*	*Adversus Judaeos*
De Praescr.	*De Praescriptione*
Adv. Prax.	*Adversus Praxeam*
De Res. Carn.	*De Resurrectione Carnis*
Theodoret, *H.E.*	*Historia Ecclesiastica*

I

THE DEVELOPMENT OF
DOCTRINE: THE NATURE
OF THE PROBLEM

'DR OWEN CHADWICK, in his book *From Bossuet to Newman*, has provided a superb historical survey of the material [relating to the question of doctrinal development] but no Anglican theologian seems to have thought the problem itself worthy of his attention.'[1] So writes Dr Mascall, charging not only my Cambridge colleagues who contributed to *Soundings* but Anglican theologians at large with this sin of omission. It is no disrespect to Dr Chadwick's scholarship to say that I find little cause for surprise that his historical researches should not have given rise to much modern theological discussion of the question of doctrinal development. The historical story is full of fascination. One reads and one admires; one admires not only the narrator of the story but also the characters within it; one admires the broad sweep of their intellectual convictions and the detailed subtlety of their individual reasonings. But it is like reading a debate about

[1] E. L. Mascall, *Up and Down in Adria* (1963), p. 13.

I

the movements of the planets before the invention of the telescope. The general problems with which they were concerned are real problems; but the particular problems to which they addressed themselves so vigorously are not ours; and, more emphatically still, the way in which they approached them is not and cannot be ours. And so it is only in the most general manner that the historical treatment points on to the theological. The study of doctrinal development is a study of importance; but the debates of the eighteenth and nineteenth centuries must not be expected to throw any great light on the road we have to tread in pursuit of it at the present time.

The most obvious of all divisions concerning the nature of doctrinal development in the life of the Church lies between those who consider all such development as has received the accredited sanction of the Church to be wholly true and those who believe it to include an element of error. Newman and his opponents within the Roman church stood on the same side of that dividing line. They were in full agreement that the development of doctrine within the Roman church was wholly and infallibly true. The issue that divided them was whether that development was to be described in purely logical or in at least partly historical terms. On the one hand stood the claim that in doctrinal definition the Church was simply making explicit

what implicitly she had always known and professed; on the other hand stood the assertion that
the process of doctrinal definition involved the
discovery of truths of which the Church had not
previously been fully conscious. If we ask what the
difference between these two views amounts to in
practice, the question is not easily answered. As the
final paragraph of Dr Chadwick's book suggests,
the questions which we want to ask of both sides are
in large measure semantic ones.[1] To the one party
we want to press questions about the nature of the
implicit but apparently unexplored beliefs of the
primitive Church of which they speak. In what
sense of the word 'logical' can the kind of development of doctrine of which we know from history
be described as exclusively logical? And to the
other group we want to press similar questions
about the nature of those unconscious inklings of
belief in the primitive Church which only rise to
the level of consciousness at a later stage. In what
sense of the word 'new' can there be genuinely new
insights which are nevertheless not new revela-
tions? These, as Dr Chadwick suggests, are the
questions to which his historical inquiry most
naturally gives rise. But it is only if we share the
underlying assumption which was common ground
to both Newman and his opponents that these will
seem the most valuable starting-points for an

[1] O. Chadwick, *From Bossuet to Newman* (1957), p. 195.

1-2

attempt to deal theologically with the question of the development of doctrine.

Within the Roman Catholic church, that basic assumption still exists. There, therefore, the debate continues along the same lines, and the questions which Dr Chadwick poses are questions of vital theological concern. It is not my purpose to try to carry Dr Chadwick's historical investigation on up to the present time. Nevertheless, the continuing debate among Roman Catholic scholars has brought to the fore one particular issue which does seem to be of paramount importance for any approach to this problem. If the deposit of faith be regarded as existing in the form of certain basic propositions, it is clearly impossible (if one accepts historical evidence as relevant at all) to escape the claim that the later formulations of dogma cannot be reached by a process of deductive logic from the original propositions and must contain an element of novelty. For this and many other reasons, scholars are increasingly prone to define the deposit of faith in broader terms. It is the *mysterium*, the person of Christ and his redemptive work, where principles other than those of deductive logic must be used.[1] 'Revelation is not the communication of a definite number of propositions . . . but an historical dialogue between

[1] H. de Lubac, 'Le problème du développement du dogme', *R.S.R.* xxxv (1948), 154–8.

4

God and man in which something happens.'[1] This emphasis is not an entirely new one. As Dr Chadwick points out, its importance—and its difficulty—emerges clearly enough from a study of Newman himself and of the obscurity attaching to his conception of Christian revelation as an idea impressed upon the corporate mind of the Church.[2] But it means that any debate about development may have to concern itself not so much with the actual process of development as with the nature of that from which the development is believed to have sprung. You cannot discuss intelligently the process of development unless you are agreed about the nature of the given starting-point from which that development begins.[3] There is not much evidence of any such agreement among theologians at the present time.

But even within the restricting confines of the view that holds all officially sanctioned developments of doctrine to be wholly and unqualifiedly true, it is doubtful whether this distinction between a purely logical understanding of doctrinal development and a broader, more historical understanding is the most important distinction that can be drawn. It certainly represents an important difference about the way in which doctrinal decisions have been reached in the past. It also

[1] K. Rahner, 'The Development of Dogma', in *Theological Investigations* (1961), 1, 48.　[2] O. Chadwick, *From Bossuet to Newman*, p. 149.
[3] Cf. H. de Lubac, *R.S.R.* xxxv, 153.

has significant implications for the way in which the Church should set about the process of determining any future defining of doctrine. But it does not directly affect our attitude towards doctrines already defined. It is therefore worth noting that there is another division of outlook with regard to the development of doctrine, still from within the ranks of those who would hold such development to be wholly true, which has a more direct bearing on our present attitude to the doctrines which have emerged from that process. This second, and in many ways more important, distinction lies between those who would regard the development of doctrine that has actually taken place in the Church as a necessary process and those who would be content to describe it in less absolutist terms as legitimate and valuable. This distinction is not identical with the one we have been discussing so far. It would be perfectly possible, for example, for someone who held a strongly historical theory of development either to regard that development as one absolutely necessary for the life of the Church or to give to it a lesser, though still positive, role in the divine economy.

The distinction that I am drawing here can be illustrated from the realm of church order, in particular from the emergence of the episcopate. There are of course those who regard that development as a perversion. But even from within the

6

ranks of those who would see it as a true development there is scope for important variation of outlook. Some will see the episcopate as already consciously embodied and expressed in the persons of the apostles. Others will look upon it as a new but entirely valid development from the clearly distinguishable stage of apostolic ministry. This represents a significant difference in the understanding of the past, but it is not the most important distinction in this sphere. More fundamental is the distinction between those who regard the episcopate as absolutely necessary to the life of the Church (and these will include some who hold it to be a genuinely new development of the post-apostolic age as well as those who see it as having been a feature of the Church from the very beginning) and those who do not so regard it. This distinction is the more important because it has obvious implications in terms of present action, which the other distinction does not have. Those who hold it to be a necessary development will seek to ensure its continuation in every situation that may arise. Those who consider it to have been a true and valuable development at the time but not a necessary one will rather ask how the functions which it fulfilled in its day can be properly fulfilled in our own. In this sense it is possible to hold something to have been a true development without regarding it as eternally immutable.

It might be argued in reply that the distinction which I have been drawing could only be applied to the realm of order but not to the realm of belief. It is not difficult to accept that a type of institution or a set of practices which were a wholly right and valuable development in one situation might not automatically be right and valuable in another. But can the same thing be said with regard to doctrine? If a doctrine is a wholly true development in one situation, must it not be equally true in all situations? Admittedly, change of environment cannot alter the truth value of a doctrinal statement, provided the words in which it is expressed retain their meaning unchanged. But that proviso is more significant than it sounds at first hearing. Not all statements are statements of the same kind. One does not need to deny all objectivity to doctrinal statements to claim that they are not statements of the most straightforward kind, capable of verification in direct sense experience. There is a complexity about the logic of doctrinal statements which means that they have their meaning only in relation to a total world-view of God and his relation to the world. And that total world-view is emphatically subject to change in differing ages. It therefore seems inescapable that what Cardinal Mercier regarded as a powerful objection to Tyrrell's modernism ought to be accepted as a simple statement of fact—' the dogmas of the Church

...change their sense, if not necessarily their expression, with the ages to which they are addressed'.[1]

It may fairly be argued in reply that such a change of sense still leaves the truth of the old doctrinal statement unaffected, for its truth or falsity can only be assessed in terms of its own world-view. The answer may be allowed and our point put in another way. A 'true' doctrinal statement (though the phrase is less simple than appears on the surface) can, it may be admitted, never lose its truth, but it can lose its relevance. A statement whose truth or falsity can be determined only in terms of a world-view that is dead and gone can hardly be a statement of direct relevance to subsequent ages; 'old formulas', to quote Loisy, 'conceived in another intellectual atmosphere no longer say what needs to be said or no longer say it suitably'.[2] And it would certainly be somewhat odd to assert that a doctrine was irrelevant, yet necessary, in the life of the Church. It does not therefore seem unreasonable to assert that some doctrines, like some institutions, may have been a true development and yet not necessary in the life of the Church outside the situation within which they were developed.

This question is no purely theoretical question. To insist upon the necessity of such doctrines

[1] G. Tyrrell, *Mediaevalism* (1908), p. 10.
[2] A. Loisy, *L'Evangile et l'Eglise* (5th edn, 1930), p. 206 (E.T.: *The Gospel and the Church* (1908), p. 216).

would be more than just a harmless anachronism. It could have a seriously inhibiting effect upon the proper task of succeeding generations.[1] To give but one example, Christian theology today is being worked out in an increasingly wide range of languages and cultures. We have to ask the question, What is the proper course of doctrinal development in African and Asiatic countries? If, for example, it be agreed that the doctrinal developments enshrined in the decision of the Council of Chalcedon with its clear enunciation of Christ as one person in two natures are necessary to the life of the Church, then they must be fully studied and used as the basis for any further development of doctrine in all parts of the world. If, on the other hand, while still regarded as a true development of Christian doctrine, they are understood as the Church's self-expression within the terms of a particular limited cultural system, then their role today will be seen in a very different guise. In that case the task of a modern African theologian will be seen not so much as building on the foundations of Chalcedon but rather as repeating the work of the early centuries within a new idiom. It is possible to regard Aristotle as having provided a valuable tool in the hands of the Church's theologians in the past without regarding that tool as indispensable for ever in the Church's execution

[1] Cf. J. N. Sanders, 'The Meaning and Authority of the New Testament', in *Soundings* (1962), p. 127.

of the dogmatic task. And this whole discussion has implications nearer home than Africa.

But the real difference between the approach to this subject which I believe to be called for today and that of men like Newman a century ago is a much more radical one. It is an unreadiness to accept in advance that doctrinal development, even within the narrowly prescribed limits of, for example, the early conciliar decisions most generally acceptable to Anglicans, can be assumed with confidence to have been wholly true in direction and in conclusion. The change which has taken place in the approach to Scripture during the same period provides a clear and close parallel. Few nowadays are prepared to claim that the divine inspiration of Scripture can only be asserted in terms of its absolute infallibility. It is true that it can, not unreasonably, be argued that there is an *a priori* case in favour of such infallibility. It is claimed, for example, by Geldenhuys that 'the fact *as such* that Jesus possesses supreme divine authority . . . gives us the assurance that the Lord of all authority would have seen to it that . . . an adequate and completely reliable account of . . . His life and work was written and preserved for the ages to come'.[1] But when he asserts that this 'follows logically' from the once-for-all nature of the revelation of God in Christ, we must demur.

[1] J. N. Geldenhuys, *Supreme Authority* (1953), p. 43.

THE MAKING OF CHRISTIAN DOCTRINE

It does not follow logically. We might have expected God to provide such a revelation, but whether he has in fact done so is something to be determined on empirical grounds. Such an empirical approach to Scripture rules out decisively any question of its infallibility. But in ruling out the infallibility of Scripture, it does not rule out the possibility of regarding it as something given by God with a positive role as a means of divine grace. The evidence suggests to us not a divinely guaranteed infallibility, but rather the outcome of an interaction of the divine Spirit with fallible human beings. And when once empiricism has led us to this point, it is perhaps not unjustifiable to claim that such a conception fits best with the whole way in which God deals with us as responsible and responsive human beings. We ought not, after all, to be too surprised at the disappointment of any *a priori* expectations of an infallible record that we may have entertained.

In the same way Newman claimed in the course of his antecedent arguments on behalf of developments in Christian doctrine that an infallible developing authority is to be expected.[1] He was ready to admit, to the dismay of some of his Catholic contemporaries, that this antecedent expectation can properly be tested against the facts of historical evidence. But his historicism was

---

[1] *Doctrine of Development* (1845), pp. 114 ff. = (1878), pp. 75 ff.

rigidly restrained—so much so in fact that many critics have denied its existence altogether.[1] When the method of historical inquiry is applied with the same kind of rigour as has been used in the case of the study of Scripture, the results would seem to be similar. Newman's infallible developing authority becomes as difficult to maintain as the infallibility of Scripture. The historical processes of doctrinal development seem as unlikely to lead to infallible decisions as the oral transmission of gospel material to lead to an infallible record of the life of Jesus. The element of human fallibility is present in the bishops and theologians of the early Church as evidently as it is in the persons of the apostles and evangelists. We have as much reason in the one case as in the other to believe either that that fallibility was totally suppressed or that it was incapable of reflecting enough of the inspiration of the divine Spirit to provide us with valuable guidance for the Church's life.

In the course of the debate about the fallibility of Scripture there was a stage at which many hoped that a satisfactory compromise solution would be reached. The Old Testament might be subject to the most radical criticism without demur; the epistles could be allowed to be the products of fallible men who were children of their own age; even in the case of the gospels the narrative sections might be admitted to contain secondary accretions.

[1] Cf. O. Chadwick, *From Bossuet to Newman*, p. 194.

But the words of Jesus, it was thought, could stand out unsullied and untouched by all such arguments. Thereby, it was hoped, the inescapable evidence of critical scholarship and the spiritual requirement of a hard core of infallible revelation would both be satisfied. But it was not to be. The isolation of the words of Jesus as a section of the scriptural record which could remain unaffected by the winds of critical scholarship blowing all around them was an impossible concept. It is not surprising that attempts of a similar kind should have been made in the field of doctrinal development. Most scholars will readily admit that much of the work of the Fathers proceeds by the normal and fallible means of conceptual argument and leads to conclusions of varying degrees of probability. This they see as essentially private interpretation of the original deposit of faith; but they will not allow it to be the whole story. In the official dogmas of the Church there must be propositions of faith which are free from this subjective and relativistic uncertainty. But the position is fundamentally the same as in the case of the Scriptures. The official dogmas of the faith are too closely related to the whole pattern of patristic thought for any such isolation to be possible. There is no more ground for regarding such a radical distinction as tenable in the case of doctrinal development than there was in the case of scriptural infallibility.

In the case of the study of Scripture we have gone a long way towards accepting the implications of such critical and empirical study. It was often a painful process; but few of us would want to go back to the security of the old fundamentalism. We know well enough that we have to study the early history of doctrinal development in the same spirit. Up to a point that is what we do. But I do not think we have fully faced the implications of our approach for our attitude to the creeds and other early formulations of doctrinal belief. As far as they are concerned we are still in the painful period of reappraisal and readjustment.

We ought not, therefore, to begin with any pre-conceived theory concerning the pattern of doc-trinal development. We can only proceed by a patient study of the historical evidence. We must trace out as carefully as we can the way in which doctrinal belief actually did develop. To do that with any thoroughness and depth of understanding is a many-sided study, in which light must be sought from a wide range of contributory fields. I do not in this book intend to say anything about such non-theological factors as imperial favour, ecclesiastical rivalries, or personal ambition. All these did have an extremely important part to play in the actual story of development. In my judge-ment they were mainly influential in determining which doctrines were accepted by what groups of people at a particular time. I do not believe that in the long run they exerted any comparably significant influence on the determination of the actual developing content of doctrinal belief itself. And it is that which is my primary concern. I have chosen rather, therefore, to begin with a study of the motives in the life of the Church which gave rise to such a development of thought. I propose next to consider some of the grounds upon which doctrinal argument was consciously based and in the light of which decisions were reached, to try to understand the reasons which led to the preference of one doctrine over another. Finally, in addition to motive and ground, I propose to consider the way in which new beliefs were expressed and related to the existing corpus of beliefs. All this must be done in the first instance with as full and as sympathetic an understanding as we can achieve of the thought-world of the early centuries. We must not too quickly impose alien criteria of judgement from the comparative detachment of our modern world. Nevertheless, in the long run something very like that is just what we have to do. If we are concerned not merely with the history of doctrinal development but with evaluating that doctrine for ourselves in the light of its historical process of development, we must raise questions about the truth and falsity of the arguments used in that process and the results achieved by it. And this we can only do from one position and with one set of criteria: that is, from the position of our contemporary world and with the criteria that seem to us appropriate to the subject-matter under review. We need, therefore, to be on the look-out for features in the story of development which, by virtue of their logical form, might tend to throw doubt upon the validity of the conclusions that stem from them.

Whether the picture which will emerge from such a study is one that will present a sufficiently coherent pattern to merit the title 'A doctrine of development' is not a question that can be decided in advance. We must be prepared to find that elements of a wholly fortuitous kind may have played a very significant part in the development which has actually taken place and that the resultant doctrinal picture may have to be adjudged a curious mixture of truth and error. We stand, after all, in the midst of a continuing process; it may be that whatever pattern of development does exist can only be seen with clarity when the process is complete.[1] But even if at the end of our study we are still unable to formulate any intellectually or aesthetically satisfying theory of development, it cannot but serve to throw some light upon the proper attitude to be taken towards doctrinal affirmations at the present time.

[1] Cf. K. Rahner, 'The Development of Dogma', p. 41: 'The *perfected* law of dogmatic development however may only be laid down when the whole unique process has reached its term.'

2

MOTIVES FOR DEVELOPMENT
IN THE PATRISTIC AGE

THE basic distinction in the whole realm of human thought is that between the self and the not-self. It is here that the baby begins as he takes his first steps in human reasoning—first steps which may be the start of a road leading to the highest pinnacles of philosophical reflexion. So the Christian Church from the very start of her life found herself forced to articulate her beliefs and practices over against the non-Christian environment in which she was set. In the course of distinguishing between the self and the not-self the baby pays particular attention to those things which appear to stand somewhere on the borderland between the two—the extremities of his body, his fingers and toes, and the gloves and socks which he finds so closely associated with them. So also with the Church: it was those who stood on the borderland between her and the distinctively non-Christian environment outside who demanded the closest attention. It was in grappling with the heretic, the would-be Christian whom she was unwilling to recognize, that the Church was forced to articulate her beliefs with an ever-increasing measure of precision. It is only as the child grows up that he begins to indulge in reasoning as a conscious activity undertaken for its own sake in comparative detachment from the stimulus of immediate need.

The analogy is admittedly fanciful. But it may be allowed to indicate three outstanding motives by which the Church was led on along the path of doctrinal development. These can be defined epigrammatically as the Church's self-understanding in relation to those outside, in relation to those half outside and half inside her borders, and finally in relation to herself. First was the apologetic motive, the need to express Christian truth in a form that would meet the requirements and answer the objections of the surrounding world. Secondly, there was the problem of heresy, the problem of those who, standing to a greater or lesser degree within the fold of the Church, yet defined the tenets of the faith in a manner which seemed to the majority wrong-headed and dangerously misleading. Thirdly (though never in isolation from the other two, since no thought is unrelated to its environment), there was the natural desire of some Christians to think out and to think through the implications of their faith as deeply and as fully as possible. We must consider in turn the way in which each of these three factors operated in the life of the Church.

Christians were a third race poised uncomfortably between the two more ancient races of Jew and Greek. Both were ready to attack—especially with the deadly weapon of ridicule—distinctively Christian ideas. The Church was therefore continually being challenged to formulate her convictions in a way which would prove less vulnerable in debate.

In the New Testament period, Jewish objections to Christian claims revolved mainly around the themes of the Messiahship of Jesus and the continuing validity of the Law. These issues were a part of the background of the life of Jesus himself. From the very beginning, therefore, Christians were forced to think out carefully the implications of the idea of a suffering Messiah and to give some definition to the role of the Law in the divine plan.

Jewish sources do not show many traces of the controversy with Christians in the years immediately after the period of the New Testament. Such evidence as there is suggests that the two main issues at stake were the divinity of Jesus and the Christian claim to be the true Israel of God. On the first of these two issues the Jewish argument was clear and straightforward. Their case rested with a massive simplicity upon the unity of God, as expressed, for example, in Isa. xliv.6: 'I am the first and the last; beside me there is no God.' Any suggestion of a divine nature attaching to the

person of Jesus would at once be opposed as in-
fringing the divine unity. The Christian had no
desire or intention to be polytheistic or even
simply ditheistic. The Old Testament Scriptures,
from which the Jewish insistence on the unity of
God was drawn, were also the Christian Scriptures.
Christian affirmations about the divinity of Christ
were therefore necessarily and naturally framed in
a way which Christians at least could feel to be
consonant with a full affirmation of the divine
unity. But the presence of Jewish controversialists
ready to pounce upon any aberration from the
narrow path of a truly monotheistic faith was an
additional stimulus in the same direction.

The second great issue was the antiquity and
continuity of Jewish faith and history. A 'new'
faith could be laughed out of court on the ground
of its novelty alone. To counter such attacks the
Christian was forced to follow up those clues in the
New Testament which had spoken of the Church
as the Israel of God. This was done in a great
variety of ways. The familiar motif of the goodness
of the younger son, in contrast to the elder, easily
lent itself to an interpretation in terms of the
superiority of the 'younger' religion of Christianity
over the 'older' religion of Judaism. The process
indeed is carried by Tertullian right back as far as
the story of Cain and Abel.[1] Thus the Christian

---

[1] *Adv. Jud.* 5.

was encouraged to develop a philosophy of history, an understanding of the Old Testament, which showed him and not the Jew as the true inheritor of all that was good in Jewish history and of all the promises of the Old Testament.

But the primary environment of the nascent Christian church was Greek rather than Jewish. And from the Greek side fundamentally similar objections were raised. The two basic complaints of the novelty of Christianity and its apparent desertion of monotheism can be found combined in a single pungent comment of Celsus. 'If these men', he writes, 'worshipped no other God but one, perhaps they would have had a valid argument. . . . But in fact they worship to an extravagant degree this man who appeared recently, and yet think it is not inconsistent with monotheism if they also worship God's servant.' It is the same two charges. Christ is one who appeared only recently —a very few years ago, says Celsus in another place; and in worshipping him Christians are either being guilty of worshipping a man or they are abandoning monotheism. Origen's reply is a vivid example of a careful doctrinal statement born of apologetic necessity. 'Therefore,' he writes, 'we worship the Father of truth and the Son who is the truth; they are two distinct existences but one in mental unity, in agreement and in identity of will.'[1]

[1] *Con. Cel.* 8. 12 (cf. also *ibid.* 1. 26).

But the Greek controversialist had many other weapons in his armoury as well. Plato had wished to banish Homer and the record of the shameful doings of his deities from his ideal republic, and later Platonism had developed the art of debunking popular religion. Much of this development was well adapted for use against the anthropomorphic ideas of the Old Testament and the whole conception of a divine incarnation. To talk of God coming down to men seemed to Celsus to imply an utterly unworthy conception of the majesty of God and to be an offence against a true understanding of God's eternal changelessness. In reply Origen declares: 'If the immortal divine Word assumed both a human body and a human soul, and by so doing appears to Celsus to be subject to change and remoulding, let him learn that the Word remains Word in essence. He suffers nothing of the experience of the body or the soul.'[1] Once again we catch a glimpse of a very significant doctrinal affirmation carefully framed to meet an apologetic need.

But the influence of the apologetic motive must not be restricted to such instances of explicit doctrinal affirmations made in reply to specific criticisms raised by a particular antagonist. The role of the apologist was not exclusively defensive. His aim was not only to find answers to particular

[1] *Con. Cel.* 4. 5 and 4. 14–15.

23

attacks; it was to convince the non-Christian of the truth of the Christian faith. Some apologists were tempted to believe that their task was best done by countering scorn with scorn and by answering ridicule with ridicule. But for the most part their concern was to commend their faith positively in a way that would seem intellectually respectable and even attractive to a cultured Greek reader. With this objective in view they were keen to stress such points of contact and of similarity as they could find between their own beliefs and the best of Greek thought. Greek philosophy, especially Plato, had said much of which they could approve. Whether, in line with earlier Jewish apologetic, they explained this as due to borrowing from the earlier work of Moses or whether, more generously, they attributed it to a partial share in the divine Logos, or whether indeed, like Justin Martyr, they did both,[1] made little difference in the long run. The important factor was their conviction that there was a common ground of shared belief to which appeal could be made.

The main area of this common ground was belief about God. The Christian's belief about Christ was something peculiarly his own, based on the empirical evidence of the incarnation and experience in the life of the Church. But belief about God was rooted in certain common notions

[1] *Apol.* 1. 46, 59.

24

(the very phrase used—κοιναὶ ἐννοίαι—is itself of Stoic origin) implanted in all men and was a real point of contact with the best thought of the ancient world. Thus Athenagoras, a Christian philosopher from Athens who wrote in the second half of the second century, can appeal to Euripides, the Pythagoreans, Plato, Aristotle, and even the Stoics as witnesses to that same unity of God which Christians affirmed.[1] At first sight such appeals might seem to have relatively little doctrinal importance. To build upon the non-Christian's already existing intimations of divinity is a natural enough form of apologetic. There seems little obvious reason why it should influence the Christian's formulation of his own beliefs. But in fact its influence was enormous. For the apologist was not arguing simply that the Greeks used the same word 'God' which was also used by Christians; he was arguing that there were points of similarity between the idea of God in Christian thought and Greek philosophy. In seeking out and stressing such points of contact between the ideas of the young Christian community and those of the long-established schools of Greek philosophy, it was almost inevitable that the former should be significantly influenced by the latter. Having described the witness of the Greek poets and philosophers to the unity of God, Athenagoras moves on

[1] Athenagoras, *Supplicatio*, 5–6.

to that of the Old Testament prophets; the latter he regards as better witnesses because they were more directly inspired (breathed upon as by the flute-player on his flute), but he does not draw any distinction between the content of their teaching about the basic issue of God's nature and the content of the philosophers' teaching.[1] Yet it is by no means clear that the affirmation that God is one has the same meaning when it appears in the course of Deutero-Isaiah's denial of the reality of the Babylonian gods that it has when it appears in the mathematical reflexions of a Pythagoras or a Plato.

The doctrinal influence of this apologetic concern is not immediately evident in the writings of the second-century apologists themselves. Their own understanding of the Christian faith is of a comparatively simple, uncomplicated kind. In general it seems to be little different from that of most of the Apostolic Fathers, men like Clement of Rome and Hermas, who belonged to the preceding generation. They give no sign that in themselves they felt any great urge to formulate more carefully the faith which they had received from their predecessors. Where they do go beyond them, it is the apologetic motive that drives them on. But, however unconsciously and unintentionally, they were in fact giving to Christian thought a new orientation; they had set the foot of the Church

[1] Athenagoras, *Supplicatio*, 7–9.

26

upon a road which would take her much further from the thought of the Apostolic Fathers than the apologists themselves could ever have conceived to be either desirable or possible. The ideas about God implicit in their approach became for their successors, Clement and Origen, part of the very substance of Christian doctrinal thinking. The case of the divine unity is a clear illustration of this tendency. Athenagoras, as we have seen, failed to distinguish between the mathematical and the prophetic conceptions of unity; but he was not himself theologian enough for the theoretical implications of that identification to appear at all fully in his own writings. But with Clement and Origen a mathematical conception of the divine unity is accepted as basic and is integrated as best it can be into their schemes of Christian theology. For Clement the idea of God is to be approached by the mathematical principle of abstraction carried to the extreme limit;[1] for Origen God is one and altogether uncompounded, one in the fullest sense that language can convey.[2]

The implications of such ideas for the whole range of Christian theology can hardly be overstated. Nothing can be more basic than one's idea of God. It is not only itself the basic Christian doctrine; it enters into and affects every other doctrine. If Clement's approach be accepted, it

[1] *Strom.* 5. 71. 2–3. [2] *Comm. Jn.* 1. 20; *De Princ.* 1. 1. 6.

establishes the negative or apophatic way as the true method of theological thinking; if Origen's definition be accepted, traditional trinitarianism is excluded from the outset. Thus ideas of the divine unity drawn from the schools of Greek philosophy came to play a great part in the development of doctrine. That they did so was not exclusively, but it was in large measure, an outcome of the Church's apologetic concern. A similar story could easily be told in terms of other attributes of God's being. But the one example will suffice to show how extensive was the influence of the apologetic motive on doctrinal development. It was not only a matter of being forced to meet particular objections levelled at Christian teaching. Its effect was more far-reaching and more deep-seated than that. It meant that all Christian thinking, and especially all Christian thinking about the being and nature of God, was influenced, often unconsciously, by philosophical ideas current in the Hellenistic world.

But the Church was faced not only with opposition and unbelief, whether scornful or sympathetic; she was faced also with what she regarded as deviation and false belief. The effect of the Church's apologetic concern on the development of doctrine was extensive though often hidden; the effect of the challenge of heresy was still more extensive and more upon the surface. The earliest theological writers of the Western church are almost wholly taken up with the answering of heresy. The whole character of Irenaeus' theology is determined by his opposition to the Gnostics with their strongly unhistorical and speculative approach towards the faith, while Marcion and Praxeas play an almost equally central role in determining the tenor of Tertullian's thought. If most of the apologists were ready to seek some common ground with their non-Christian readers, one might anticipate that writings directed towards men who at least professed some kind of faith in Christ would be even more likely to follow a similar line. But that is very far from being the case. A modern writer may declare that a heretic is a brother in Christ because only a Christian can be a heretic,[1] but that is not how the early Church saw him. Any Christian flavour attaching to the concept of the heretic was not regarded as something in his favour—rather the reverse. The heretic is like Judas, who called Christ Rabbi and kissed him;[2] and as Judas is to be classed with Caiaphas rather than with the apostles, but indeed is worse than Caiaphas by virtue of the element of treachery which attaches to his case, so the heretic is not a straying brother but the deadliest and most

[1] L. A. Zander, *Vision and Action* (1952), pp. 101–2 (cited by H. E. W. Turner, *The Pattern of Christian Truth* (1954), p. 97).
[2] Origen, *Matt. Comm. Ser.* 100; Athanasius, *Or. Con. Ar.* 3. 28.

treacherous of all opponents. If the note of scorn and ridicule is seldom absent for very long from the pen of even the more sympathetic apologists, the note of bitter vituperation is hardly ever silent for a moment in the writings against heresy.

But vituperation was never enough. The heretic claimed to be expressing Christian truth and his claim had to be met. In most cases the heretic's affirmations were on subjects about which the majority had no clearly formulated conviction; in many cases they were on subjects about which it was not unreasonable to claim that no clearly formulated conviction was possible. In answer to Gnostic speculations about the nature of the heavenly realm before the creation of the world, Irenaeus replies that such questions are unanswerable and must be left in the hand of God. The words of the prophet 'Who shall declare his generation?' are evidence of the fruitlessness of attempting to define the generation of the Logos.[1] But such a policy of silence could not be sustained for long. It could too easily be interpreted as an abdication in favour of the heretics. In the years after Irenaeus the Church's scholars did undertake to discuss at considerable length the true nature of the Son's generation. Indeed, a century and a half later, when the Council of Sirmium included in its statement of the faith the same text from

---

[1] *Adv. Haer.* 2. 28.

Isaiah which Irenaeus had used with the self-same intention of excluding all claims to knowledge about the nature of the Son's generation, that statement was described by Hilary as the Blasphemy of Sirmium, a Compulsory Ignorance Act commanding men to be ignorant of what they already knew.[1]

The same story could be repeated many times over. The orthodox church leader declares the faith as he knows it and insists that further definition is inappropriate to the nature of the subject. But the mind of man is congenitally unwilling to accept such apparently arbitrary limitations on the bounds of possible knowledge and understanding. Some Christians therefore claim to be able to define that aspect of the faith more fully, but do so in a way that proves unacceptable to the main body of the Church. So, choosing the lesser of two evils, the next generation of church leaders define with care what their predecessors in the faith declared to be by nature incapable of being defined. One example will suffice. Cyril of Jerusalem declared in his Catechetical Lectures delivered about A.D. 350 that it is enough to acknowledge the identity of the gifts of the Father and of the Holy Spirit, but that the nature and the substance of that Holy Spirit are not proper subjects of inquiry.[2] Ten years later the attention of Athanasius was called to a group of Egyptian

---

[1] *De Synodis*, 10. [2] *Cat.* 16. 24.

Christians who, while accepting the full divinity of the Son, spoke disparagingly of the Spirit as a creature; as a result of their errors he found himself forced to launch out on just such an inquiry into the nature of the Spirit as Cyril had discouraged, even though he had no clear terminology in which to discuss his subject-matter with any measure of precision.[1] But the Tropici, as this Egyptian group were named by Athanasius, were not alone. There were others all over the Eastern world who followed a similar line of thought. They readily acknowledged the Son's divinity but, with varying degrees of definiteness, rejected any suggestion of the Spirit's godhead. So under pressure of these *Pneumatomachoi* or Spirit-Fighters, as the orthodox called them, still further exactness of definition was felt to be required, and within another twenty years the doctrine of the Holy Spirit's procession within the godhead had been developed by Gregory of Nazianzus and incorporated in the Creed of Constantinople of A.D. 381.

Thus the leaders of the Church were forced by the presence of heretical ideas into an ever-increasing precision of doctrinal teaching. In the words of Hilary they could say: 'The errors of heretics and blasphemers force us to deal with unlawful matters, to scale perilous heights, to speak unutterable words, to trespass on forbidden

[1] Cf. *Ep. ad Ser.* 4. 2–3.

ground. Faith ought in silence to fulfil the commandments, worshipping the Father, reverencing
with him the Son, abounding in the Holy Spirit,
but we must strain the poor resources of our
language to express thoughts too great for words.
The error of others compels us to err in daring to
embody in human terms truths which ought to be
hidden in the silent veneration of the heart.'[1]

Thus it was often the heretic who determined
the general lines along which doctrine should
develop; it was he who chose the ground on which
the doctrinal battles were to be fought. Frequently indeed he chose not only the ground for
the battle but also the weapons to be used in it. To
generations of Christians the description of the
Son as 'of one substance' with the Father has
served as a joyous affirmation of faith in a creed
sung at one of the highest moments of Christian
worship. Yet that is very far from being the way
in which it found entrance into the vocabulary of
Christian doctrine. Rather it was admitted with
reluctance as being the only available means of
excluding Arianism. Athanasius insists more than
once that the root of Arian error lies in its replacement of the scriptural idea of God as Father with
the philosophical idea of God as unoriginated
being. It is the Arians, therefore, he argues, who
made necessary the Church's use of the unscriptural

[1] Hilary, *De Trinitate*, 2. 2.

term *homoousios*, the Greek word introduced into the creed at Nicaea and familiarly rendered in English by the phrase 'of one substance with'. They had used unscriptural language to bring in unscriptural ideas; such ideas could only be countered by language of the same philosophical kind which gave clear and unequivocal expression to the true scriptural sense.[1]

What Athanasius claims here seems substantially to be justified. Indeed his case can be stated in still more precise and rigorous form. The word *ousia* (substance or being) has become one of the most fundamental of all theological terms. It does not occur in the New Testament—except to describe the Father's substance which was squandered by the prodigal son. It occurs occasionally in writers before the time of Arius but not with any precise or technical meaning. By Origen it can be used to express either what the Father and the Son have in common or that in respect of which they differ.[2] Arius seems to be the first to give to it a precise and significant role in his scheme of thought. He insists with great emphasis that the distinction between the Father and the Son is one of *ousia*. That distinction is basic and fundamental to all his thought. It is for him the necessary means of giving expression to the essential tran-

[1] *De Decretis*, 19, 28; *Or. Con. Ar.* 1. 34; *Ad Afros*, 7.
[2] Contrast the use of *ousia* in *De Oratione*, 15, with that in *Comm. Jn.* 10. 37.

scendence of the Father over everything else, including the Son. If that distinction be once granted,
he is as ready as anyone else to speak of the
revelatory function of the Son as the Father's
image or of the similarity of character and will
existing between Father and Son.[1] If this be at
all a true description of Arius' position, it is clear
that it could only be countered by some opposing
affirmation concerning the divine *ousia*. Any other
line of argument would leave Arius' fundamental
position unaffected. The choice of *ousia* language
as the terminology in which the Church's doctrine
of the godhead was to be worked out was really,
therefore, the choice of Arius.

But the point can be made more specific still.
What is true of *ousia* language in general seems
also to be true of the word *homoousios* in particular.
In his letter to Alexander, Arius had described the
word as Manichaean, apparently implying that it
involved a false use of physical categories in thought
about the nature of the godhead; moreover,
Eusebius of Nicomedia is reported to have used
the term as a kind of *reductio ad absurdum* in
speaking of the relation of the Son to the Father
in a letter produced early on at the Council of
Nicaea itself. Ambrose, who records the story of
Eusebius, declares that 'the Fathers put this word
in their exposition of the faith because they saw it

---

[1] See my 'In Defence of Arius', *J.T.S.* n.s. XIII (1962), 345.

3-2

daunted their adversaries'. He may well be right.
The most satisfactory explanation of the introduction of the word *homoousios* into the formulary of
Nicaea is that the Arians were thoroughly com-
mitted to its rejection in advance. It was not only
ousia language in general but *homoousios* itself for
which Arius was ultimately responsible.[1]

The influence of heresy on the early development
of doctrine is so great that it is almost impossible
to exaggerate it. Yet what is almost impossible can
still be done. It would be an exaggeration if we
were to accept as the whole truth Hilary's picture
of the early Fathers as the reluctant theologians.
In any community of people there are always some
who will seek naturally and spontaneously to
develop the intellectual and philosophical aspects
of its life. Even though the Church may not have
included many wise according to worldly stan-
dards, as St Paul admits, and though many of
the early Christians may have been ignorant, stupid
and uneducated, as Celsus accuses them of being,
yet there were those among their number for
whom the spirit of inquiry was a living and natural
impulse.

Irenaeus' advocacy of a policy of silence has
much to commend it when answering the wilder
speculations of the Gnostics, but not even for him

[1] See my 'ὁμοούσιος ἡμῖν', *J.T.S.* n.s. xvi (1965), 454-61.

was it ever the whole story. Tertullian may argue that faith is enough, that the Church has nothing in common with the Academy, that one who has Christ has no need of curiosity, and that inquiry is ruled out once the gospel has come,[1] but even he is not always true to his own fideist convictions. Though he denounces philosophy as the root of all heresy, his own debt to Stoic thought is considerable. A negative reaction to heresy was never enough. Even a counter-statement of doctrinal belief on the ground and in the terms chosen by heresy was not the Church's last word. There is no smoke without fire. Even the speculations of the Gnostics were more than the idle imaginings of empty minds. The heretic was concerned with real problems. In the long run the Christian answer had to come from those who, whether they admitted it or not, shared the heretic's intellectual concern and sought to answer the same problems in their own way.

Such a spirit is most fully exemplified in the work of Clement and Origen. Clement agrees with Tertullian that curiosity as such is no proper motive for the Christian thinker. Intellectual inquiry is one aspect of Christian consecration. Clement's ideal, the Christian Gnostic, is not simply the Christian intellectual. The knowledge which characterizes him is one that has grown

[1] *De Praescr.* 7.

out of faith and is intimately associated with love. Yet in this knowledge every form of human reasoning has a part to play. Clement is never tired of asserting that all truth is one. He admits that man's search for truth has sometimes led him astray, but argues that that has been because it has been carried on without reference to Christ or that it has been a result of the distorting and perverting influence of sin. The Christian has no need to be afraid of inquiry, of the genuine search for the truth. The words of Jesus in declaring 'I am the truth' can properly be applied to the truth for which the philosopher seeks. Thus the spirit of inquiry rightly understood is for Clement no enemy of revelation. It is a right and proper part of that total obedience which man owes to God.

In the preface to his *De Principiis* Origen describes the role of speculative thought and defines it as having a twofold function. In the first place, it may be used to supply a unified synthesis of the dogmatic utterances of the basic tradition. To show in this way the reasonableness of the Christian truths as forming a single coherent body of doctrine is a fitting task for the thoughtful Christian—indeed it is one imposed on him by Scripture in the words of Hos. x. 12 (in the Septuagint version): 'Enlighten yourselves with the light of knowledge.' In the second place, the tradition did not set out to be a complete and comprehensive statement of

Christian doctrine. It was rather an irreducible minimum on matters of universal import. There were many other subjects not covered by the basic tradition. On these it was permissible and in fact desirable to exercise the speculative mind, provided it was always recognized that conclusions on such matters must be regarded as tentative and lacking the definiteness of the basic tradition itself.

On another occasion Origen speaks of moral discipline as the dull, but necessary, body-building bread of life, and of speculation as the wine, which also gives nourishment but still more gives enjoyment and exhilaration.[1] The image is an excellent picture of his own attitude and of his own practice. He regards the spirit of inquiry as something of positive value; still more patently he finds in it something of positive enjoyment. If he is himself unquestionably the supreme example of such a passion in the early Church, there were others who shared it (sometimes indeed unconsciously) to a lesser degree. Such a spirit never operated in isolation from the external impetus of apologetic or heresy. None of the early Fathers enjoyed the academic seclusion of a modern university lecture-room. The influence of this spirit in the field of doctrinal development cannot therefore be illustrated as directly as in the other two cases. But any account of the motives of that

[1] *Comm. Jn.* I. 30.

development which left out altogether the motive of thinking through the full implications of the faith for its own sake (or, as Clement would have put it, for Christ's sake) would be both incomplete and misleading.

Uncovering the motives which prompt a man to pursue a particular line of thought does nothing to determine the truth or falsity of his conclusions. This study of the motives which led the Church along the road of doctrinal development cannot settle the question of the validity of the doctrines thereby developed. The truth or otherwise of those doctrines depends upon the validity of the reasoning by which they were determined. It is to that that we must now turn. The value of this examination of motives consists in the help that it can give us in securing a more vivid and more accurate understanding of the arguments which were used. In that way it can serve to help indirectly in the task of evaluating the achievement of early doctrinal thinking which is our ultimate goal in this study.

3

SCRIPTURE AS A SOURCE
OF DOCTRINE

SCRIPTURE as a source of Christian doctrine
—it is tempting for one nurtured in the
Reformed tradition to change the indefinite
article into the definite. Is not *sola scriptura* the
ground of Christian truth? Would it not therefore
be truer to speak of Scripture as *the* source of
Christian doctrine? However great one's sympathy
with the concept of *sola scriptura* as a dogmatic
principle, such a change would clearly falsify the
facts with which we are here concerned and would
also obscure the primary purpose of this section of
our inquiry. It would falsify the facts because the
emergence of the Scriptures and the development
of doctrine were not successive stages in Christian
history; in the earliest period of that history the
two processes went on simultaneously. Scripture
in the sense in which we use that word today could
not be the source of the earliest developments in
Christian doctrine for the very obvious reason that
it was not then in existence in its present form to
fulfil that role. But the change from speaking of
Scripture as *a* source of Christian doctrine to

speaking of it as *the* source would also obscure my intention in another way. To speak of it as the source of Christian doctrine would suggest to our minds the general content of the biblical revelation as a whole, but I shall be more concerned in this chapter with the influence of the written form upon the way in which doctrine developed. The basic questions with which I want to deal are the questions, What was the effect upon the development of doctrine of the fact that the content of the revelation came to be recorded in specific documents? and What was the effect of the particular way in which those documents were regarded and interpreted?

The Church was never without Scriptures of some kind. In 1 Cor. xv, Paul reminds his readers of the fundamentals of the gospel which he had preached to them. These include not merely the bare facts of Christ's death and resurrection, but also the affirmation that they had happened 'in accordance with the Scriptures'. Thus from the very start the Old Testament Scriptures took their place as an essential element in the Christian message to be proclaimed. The substance of the faith was not simply the facts of Christ's life, death and resurrection, but those facts understood in the light of Old Testament Scripture. Thus Scripture, in the form of the Old Testament, was from the very outset a significant source of Christian doctrine.

But the more specifically Christian content of the faith, both the historical facts and the pattern of their interpretation, was at first a matter not of written record but rather of oral transmission. For a long time, even after many of the New Testament writings had been written, the method of oral transmission continued to be regarded as the basic way in which the substance of the Christian gospel was to be learned and passed on. Papias, bishop of Hierapolis in Asia Minor in the first half of the second century, is not unrepresentative of his age in preferring to the written record of books a living and abiding voice, a continuous chain of remembered teaching which could be traced back to 'the commandments given by the Lord to faith, and reaching us from the Truth himself'.[1] The overall picture to be found in the writings of Justin Martyr and the other apologists contemporary with him is fundamentally similar; their conception of Christianity is the teaching of Jesus spreading its way around the world through the medium of the preaching first of the apostles and then of those who came after them.

Many factors, however, combined to ensure that in the long run the New Testament writings should come to play an immeasurably bigger part in the development of Christian doctrine than a study of mid-second-century Christian authors might lead

[1] Eusebius, *H.E.* 3. 39. 3-4.

43

one to anticipate. With the passage of time the importance of the written record as opposed to oral testimony for the transmission of the facts about Jesus was bound to increase. Justin himself records that the memoirs of the apostles were included in the regular worship of the Church alongside the reading of the Old Testament Scriptures. Such a practice could not help but enhance their standing in the life of the Church as a whole. But the vital factor in the growing emphasis on the written records of the New Testament was the prevalence of Gnosticism. Those who had to deal with the vagaries of Gnostic secret traditions and apocryphal writings became increasingly aware of the importance of well-authenticated written records. Men like Irenaeus did much to promote the idea of New Testament Scriptures, standing alongside the Old, as a clear-cut entity with commanding authority in the life of the Church.

Yet Scripture was never for Irenaeus *sola scriptura*, Scripture as an isolated phenomenon. Just as the apostolic succession of bishops is for him simply an important focus in the essential succession of the public life of the Church and could not conceivably be thought of by him as something that could exist as a chain of *episcopi vagantes* away from the main stream of the Church's life, so also Scripture does not for him stand as an

44

independent authoritative record on its own. Scripture and tradition go together, not as two distinct things but as interlocking parts of a single reality. Irenaeus' insistence upon the two is an insistence that Scripture is not to be read as an independent book, whose message is entirely unknown, but as a book whose fundamental theme is already known, because that fundamental theme is the living faith of the Church by which the Christian already lives.

But however much Irenaeus may have insisted upon such a close interrelation of Scripture and tradition, the emergence at the close of the second century of a generally recognized set of authoritative documents was of immense significance. The source of the Christian revelation was God himself. Of that there had never been any doubt. The tradition which had been handed down in the life of the Church had been conceived as deriving from the apostles, who had received it from Christ, who in his turn had received it from God. But as long as it was a matter of oral tradition there was room for a measure of flexibility—room, indeed, as experience had shown, for a measure of flexibility too great to be tolerated. So it had proved necessary for that revelation to be recorded in authoritative writings. The author of the revelation was the same, none other than God Himself. Christians therefore believed themselves to have within their hands a written record whose ultimate author was God. Once such a conviction was firmly established, Scripture was bound to be the primary conscious source for all subsequent doctrine.

This belief that God was the ultimate author of all Scripture was independent of any theology of inspiration, any theory about the method by which that authorship had been effected in practice. This was not a subject with which the Fathers were very much concerned. Much has been made of the words of Athenagoras, who speaks of the prophets as 'lifted in ecstasy above the natural operations of their minds by the impulses of the divine Spirit', and 'of the Spirit making use of them as a flute-player breathes into a flute'.[1] But the saying refers only to the Old Testament prophets and is not sufficiently representative to deserve being described as 'the dominant theory of inspiration' for Scripture as a whole in the thought of the Fathers.[2] This kind of language is not commonly used at all of the New Testament writings,[3] and even with regard to the Old Testament prophets other early Christian writers are to be found explicitly distinguishing the nature of the prophets' inspiration from ecstatic experiences involving a loss of rational consciousness.[4]

[1] *Supplicatio*, 9.
[2] As by A. M. Ramsey, 'The Authority of the Bible', in Peake's *Commentary on the Bible* (ed. M. Black, 1962), p. 5.
[3] R. P. C. Hanson, *Tradition in the Early Church* (1962), p. 211.
[4] E.g. Origen, *Con. Cel.* 7. 3-4.

But all such issues were secondary. The important point, about which no element of doubt was felt, was that the ultimate author was God and that therefore, when the true meaning of the text was once grasped, that meaning was God's and not just man's. From this basic fact about the ultimate authorship of Scripture two principles followed, the unity of the whole and the significance of detail, since God can neither be inconsistent with himself nor do anything without a purpose. These two principles of expecting consistency and of paying attention to detail are sensible and important principles for the guidance of any interpreter, but both are capable of being seriously overworked. In the third and fourth centuries both were seriously overworked. We must consider each of them more closely.

The point at which the consistency of Scripture was most obviously open to attack was in terms of the evident differences between the Old and New Testaments. Christians were under attack on this score on two fronts. On the one hand the Jew could argue that the Old Testament prophecies looked forward to a glorious and conquering Messiah, while the New Testament drew a picture of one who was by contrast weak and utterly unworthy. On the other hand, when Marcion emphasized the contrast between the two Testaments it was in a manner designed to denigrate the

Old. In his eyes the differences between the two were so great that they must be speaking of two different 'Gods', that of the Old being character-ized by a harsh and punitive justice, that of the New by love and goodness.

From the beginning Christians had believed that the Old and the New helped to illuminate and confirm one another. The facts of Christ's death and resurrection were only seen as properly Christian facts when they were seen to be 'accord-ing to the Scriptures'. This was the theme of the first Christian sermon. 'This is that which was spoken by the prophet Joel ...' (Acts ii. 16). Peter insists that the strange happenings of Pentecost could only be understood when seen in relation to the prophecy of Joel that in the last days God would pour out of his Spirit upon all flesh. But similarly the Old Testament is illuminated by its fulfilment in the New. As 2 Peter puts it (i. 16–19), those who have been eye-witnesses of Christ's majesty have the prophetic word made more sure; or, as Origen writes, 'before the advent of Christ it was not altogether possible to provide clear proofs of the divine inspiration of the ancient Scriptures; but Christ's coming led those who might suspect the law and the prophets not to be divine to the clear conviction that they were composed by the aid of heavenly grace'.[1] Thus the

[1] *De Princ.* 4. 1. 6.

interrelation of the two Testaments was a basic axiom of orthodox thought. One might almost claim that in the second century it was the primary criterion in terms of which orthodoxy is to be defined. When, for example, Clement of Alexandria wishes to defend the authority of Paul against those who are doubtful or critical of it, he does so by insisting that Paul's teaching is in full accord with that of the Old Testament.[1]

But if this basic axiom was to be successfully maintained under pressure, it clearly needed to be elaborated and worked out in greater detail. Indeed it could only be done with the comprehensiveness that the contemporary situation required with the aid of a thorough-going allegorical interpretation of the Old Testament in particular, but also of the New. Thus and only thus could an unbreakable unity between the two Testaments be achieved; but it was achieved at a heavy price. For the unbreakable unity thus achieved was a unity without diversity, in which the newness of the New Testament was obscured, if not denied altogether.

The primary outcome of this minimizing of the difference between the two Testaments was an illegitimate reading back into the Old Testament of Christian ideas drawn in reality from the New. Such allegorization of the Old Testament has important repercussions for the student of exegesis;

[1] *Strom.* 4. 134. 2.

it is relatively unimportant for the student of doctrine. But this kind of evening out of the differences between the two Testaments did not always work in the same direction. It could result not only in a Christianizing of the Old Testament but also in a Judaizing of the New. Ignatius had insisted to those who sought to refute him from the text of the Old Testament that his one criterion was Christ, his cross and resurrection; the Old Testament was relevant to the understanding of Christian doctrine but for that purpose its voice must address us not directly but only indirectly, passing through the transforming prism of Christ himself.[1] But many of those who followed Ignatius failed to draw the distinction which he made. If the whole of Scripture be the words of God, then God speaks to us through it all equally. This meant that for the less allegorically minded in particular there was always a danger that the voice of Scripture would speak in Old Testament tones in a way which might lack the distinctively Christian note. The outstanding example of this kind is the way in which Paul's teaching about a radical freedom from the curse of the law was tamed in order to make it as wholly consistent as possible with the straightforward teaching of the Old Testament. Another example, less widely recognized but equally far-reaching in its effects, is

[1] *Philadelphians*, 8–9.

Cyprian's teaching about the Christian ministry. It is well known that in the discussions about the role and function of the ministry which figure so largely in the short but troubled period of his episcopate Cyprian frequently quotes from Old Testament teaching about the Jewish priesthood. A careful study of his writings shows that these quotations are of much more than purely illustrative significance; they are the main ground upon which his ideas are based.[1]

The second great principle of interpretation, which also followed directly from the conviction that God was the ultimate author of all Scripture, was the principle of the significance of detail. In Gal. iii. 16 Paul bases an argument for his Christological interpretation of the promise to Abraham recorded in Genesis on the fact that the promise is to his 'seed' (in the singular) rather than to 'seeds' (in the plural). Much of the detailed interpretation of the Fathers is in similar vein. The most unimportant and unintentional details of the text are regarded as significant and are given great emphasis in the course of interpretation. Exegesis of this kind is to be found in the discussion of doctrinal matters as fully as in other contexts. A striking example may be cited from the Arian controversy.

---

[1] For the evidence on which this judgement is based, see my 'Theological Legacy of St Cyprian', *J.E.H.* xiv (1963), 144–7. Cf. also S. L. Greenslade, 'Scripture and other Doctrinal Norms in Early Theories of the Ministry', *J.T.S.* xliv (1943), 171–6.

The words of Wisdom in Prov. viii. 22, 'The Lord created me at the beginning of his work', were an important proof-text in Arian argumentation. They were seen not as a rough prefigurement of Christological truth but as a precise indication of the Son's created status. Athanasius goes to great length to show that Arius has misinterpreted the verse, but it never occurs to him to suggest that the text is irrelevant to the determination of the issue at stake. Although it is a text which clearly fits the Arian system better than his own, he accepts it as a legitimate test and indulges in the most complex and at times inconsistent exegesis to avoid the Arian implications of the words.[1] Moreover, he uses the same kind of Old Testament text in the same kind of way in support of his own case. He in his turn can cite as evidence of the uncreated nature of the Son the words of Ps. cx. 3: 'From the dew of the morning I begat thee before the morning star.'[2] But although debate about such scriptural texts played a considerable role in the course of the controversy, they did not play a directly determinative role in the doctrinal conviction of either side. Arius did not come to believe that the Son was 'created' because he found that word used of Wisdom in Prov. viii. 22; the text was secondary support for a belief primarily based on quite other philosophical grounds. Similarly,

[1] Athanasius, *Or. Con. Ar.* 2. 18–82.   [2] *De Decretis*, 13, 21.

Athanasius did not come to believe that the Son was 'begotten' because he found the word used in Ps. cx. The role of Scripture here was rather confirmatory of a position originally adopted for quite other reasons. That may be to reduce its significance in such cases; it is not to destroy it altogether. For the ability to find apparently precise and detailed confirmation of one's own convictions in the exact wording of Scripture was not the insincere or artificial production of an additional weapon for use against one's enemies; it was a genuine and psychologically important reinforcement of one's own beliefs.

A similar verdict, that the role of Scripture was secondary but still significant, applies to the great majority of cases where doctrinal argument is apparently based on this kind of appeal to detail. Origen argues that the word 'man' in the words of Jesus, 'Now you seek to kill me, a man who told you the truth' (John viii. 40), and in the words of Caiaphas, 'It is expedient that one man should die for the people' (John xi. 50), is doctrinally significant. It is indicative of the fact that it is only the human Jesus and not the divine Word who dies.[1] But his conviction of the need to distinguish sharply here between the humanity and the divinity of Christ is based on his belief in the divine impassibility, his conviction that suffering cannot properly be ascribed to God, rather than on the

[1] Origen, *Comm. Jn.* 28. 18.

particular form of the scriptural text. This is clearly borne out by the fact that he fully acknowledges that Scripture does not always appear to speak with the doctrinal precision which such a method of interpretation presupposes. Scripture, indeed, is inconvenient enough to speak on occasion of the dying of the Son of God. But this does not lead Origen to abandon his belief in divine impassibility or his conviction that it is the human Jesus only who dies. In such cases he applies the principle of interpretation known as *communicatio idiomatum* or the sharing of properties, according to which it was claimed that in view of the unity existing between the two natures in the one Christ Scripture could in fact apply to one nature what in strict logic referred only to the other.[1] Thus, whatever the actual text of Scripture, Origen was always able to deduce the same doctrinal understanding of Christ's two natures. Apollinarius, who denied that Christ had a human mind, used the famous Johannine incarnation text that the Word became *flesh* in support of that denial.[2] But it is evident from the tenor of his teaching as a whole that directly exegetical arguments of this kind were not the real grounds of his conviction; the real reason which led him to adopt the position which he took was his belief that for the divine Word to be

[1] Origen, *De Princ.* 2. 6. 3.
[2] E.g. H. Lietzmann, *Apollinaris und seine Schule* (1904), Frag. 2 (p. 204).

conjoined in one person with a human mind would
be psychologically inconceivable and soteriologi-
cally disastrous.[1] Augustine taught that all men
sinned in Adam, and used the Latin text of Rom.
v. 12 (*in quo omnes peccaverunt*: 'in whom all have
sinned') in support. This rendering he derived
from an earlier Latin commentator, Ambrosiaster,
but it simply cannot stand as an interpretation of
the Greek text. The Greek phrase (ἐφ' ᾧ), which
is literally but unidiomatically translated by the
Latin phrase *in quo*, could not (as the Latin could)
bear the meaning 'in whom' (A.V. margin); it can
only mean 'because' or 'for that' (A.V.). But if
Augustine had been aware of that fact and had
thereby been deprived of the support of Rom.
v. 12, his beliefs about original sin would not have
collapsed altogether. Their real basis lies else-
where. In general terms it lies in a true apprehension of the moral solidarity of the human race, of
the fact that in our moral actions and our moral
failures we are inescapably influenced by one
another. More specifically it lies in what has been
called the principle of seminal identity, the principle that a man is in some real sense embodied in
his ancestors because as seed he is already latent
within them; if Levi can be said to have paid tithes
to Melchizedek because he was present in the loins of
his forefather, Abraham, who did so (Heb. vii. 9–10),

---

[1] See pp. 97–8 below.

then all men can be said to have sinned in Adam since he is the forefather of all. Once again the precise exegesis of Rom. v. 12 is secondary support for Augustine's doctrinal belief, not its true foundation.[1]

One final example may be given where the appeal to the wording of Scripture seems possibly to have played a decisive role at a critical moment in the course of doctrinal development. The doctrine concerned is the question whether or not Christ possessed a human soul. It is well known that this issue became a matter of direct debate only in the later decades of the fourth century in reaction to the teaching of Apollinarius. But that was not the beginning of the story. Tertullian and Origen had both clearly affirmed the fact of Christ's human soul. Origen, indeed, had given to that soul a very special place as the means through which the union of divine Logos and human flesh was brought about. It was for him a kind of middle term which softened the harshness of the direct conjunction suggested by the concept of the incarnation of the divine Word. But to the majority of those who followed him in the Eastern church such a conception of Christ's human soul seemed to detract from the full reality of the incarnation and from the unity of Christ's person. The extreme develop-

[1] Cf. the judgements of J. F. Bethune-Baker, *Early History of Christian Doctrine* (2nd edn, 1920), p. 309, n. 2, and of G. I. Bonner, *Augustine of Hippo* (1963), pp. 372–4.

ment of the ideas implicit in Origen by Paul of Samosata with his picture of the impersonal divine Logos conjoined to a full human Jesus had a decisive impact on the thinking of the majority. In the light of Paul of Samosata's teaching they came to feel that there was no place for a human soul in any adequate understanding of Christ's person. This outlook represented the general view of the Eastern church in the closing years of the fourth century. It was common ground alike to Arius and Athanasius and must be recognized as such for any satisfactory understanding of the nature of the debate between them. None the less, the belief that Christ had a human soul was never made the subject of direct attack or official condemnation, and thereby a way was more easily left open for its eventual restoration as the formal view of the Church. We may well ask why it was that if opposition to the idea of Christ's possession of a human soul was so widespread and so strong, it never came to the point of overt denial or denunciation.

Two pieces of evidence suggest that at least one important reason was that the text of Scripture spoke of the soul of Christ. In the early years of the fourth century Pamphilus composed a work in defence of Origen. On most issues he is the wholehearted champion of Origen against his critics, but he seems to regard the objection that Origen speaks of Christ's human soul as one of the more reasonable complaints being raised against his memory. He does not deny the charge nor does he argue directly for the truth of Origen's belief. Instead, he simply declares that Scripture talks in the same way of Christ's soul, and that Origen is hardly to be blamed for using language which is, after all, the language of Scripture.[1]

Further confirmation that it was the text of Scripture which kept alive the concept of Christ's human soul at a time when the main trend of theological thought was strongly opposed to it is to be found in the writings of Pamphilus' collaborator in the defence of Origen, Eusebius of Caesarea. He not only makes no use of the idea of Christ's human soul in his own theological writing, but comes very much nearer than other writers of the same period to outright denial of it.[2] But in spite of this there are occasions when he does use the term; those occasions, as de Riedmatten points out, are always closely related to comment on the biblical text.[3]

In this instance, therefore, the precise wording of the scriptural text does seem to have played a more vital role in the determination of how doctrine developed. It was not on this occasion a matter of the text of Scripture providing confirmation

[1] *Apologia pro Origene*, 5 (*P.G.* 17 590 ab).
[2] H. de Riedmatten, *Les Actes du Procès de Paul de Samosate*, pp. 68–81.
[3] *Ibid.* p. 78, n. 75, where detailed references are given.

for doctrinal beliefs already determined on other broader grounds. It was a question of the text of Scripture competing against the contemporary trend of doctrinal thought and holding that trend in check. The decisive influence which led in the end to the Church's insistence against Apollinarius on the fact of Christ's possession of a human soul was admittedly not the bare text of Scripture. It was rather the theological principle that Christ must have had a human soul for our human souls to be redeemed. None the less, it remains true that it was the text of Scripture which played an extremely important role in the early years of the fourth century in keeping the matter open in such a way that the Church's final decision could be reached without any overt repudiation of the views of the preceding century.[1]

Ever after the early years of the second century, Scripture was so much the accepted ground of doctrinal debate and decision that it is not possible in a single chapter to do more than indicate selectively some characteristics of its role as a source of doctrine. Much of the doctrinal work of the early centuries is grounded on the evidence of Scripture in a way to which no exception can be taken. It embodies a recognition of the unity of Scripture which avoids the one-sidedness of a

See my 'The Nature of the Early Debate about Christ's Human Soul', *J.E.H.* XVI (1965), 139-51.

Marcion or a Valentinus; it shows that concern for detail without which the work even of great minds can be seriously vitiated. Were that not the case, the doctrinal decisions of the period could hardly have served the Church as fruitfully as they have done in subsequent ages. All this has not been my primary emphasis in this chapter, yet that should not be taken as suggesting that I doubt its truth or underestimate its importance. But it is not the whole truth about the way in which Scripture served as a source of doctrine in those early years. We do no service to the cause of truth by laying claim to a perfection in the development of doctrine which was never there. If we are to hold fast to the true, we must be able to distinguish the false. The emphasis on the unity of the whole Bible and the concern for detail could, as I have tried to show, be used in ways which we cannot but regard as wholly invalid. In the majority of cases the appeals to Scripture of this kind, even when used in doctrinal debate, were illustrative rather than determinative in their function. But that is not always so. It is not always possible to draw a precise line between the illustrative and the determinative uses of Scripture. The determination of doctrine was never a purely deductive task based on the bare words of Scripture. Other factors always entered in as well. But there do seem to be some cases where the appeal to Scripture was a major factor in the development of some doctrine and where the nature of that appeal is wholly unacceptable today. It is important that we be ready to admit such cases and that by patient study we learn to distinguish and, as far as possible, to isolate them. For thereby the truth of the general pattern of the development of doctrine will be enabled to stand out the more clearly.

4
LEX ORANDI

I T is not always easy to remember that theologians say their prayers and take their part in
the worship of the Church. We are most likely
to overlook this basic fact when we read some of
the more harshly polemical writings of the early
Fathers. Yet many of them were bishops, not
merely participants but leaders in the liturgical life
of the Church. And the fiercer the controversy in
which they were involved, the more important it
is to recall the influence of the Church's worship
upon their doctrinal beliefs. For it is often there
that the key to understanding the fervour and the
bitterness of the controversy lies. Men do not
normally feel so deeply over matters of formal
doctrinal statement unless those matters are felt
to bear upon the practice of their piety. The close
interrelation of doctrine and worship is an important element in explaining the desperate seriousness
with which issues of doctrine were regarded in the
early centuries.

The importance of the early Church's worship
as a clue to the understanding of many features of
the New Testament has been much stressed in
recent years. The main emphasis in such studies

has lain upon liturgical practice as helping to explain the way in which different New Testament writings have come to take their present form. But the practice of worship is almost equally important for any study of doctrinal development within the New Testament period. Two examples may serve to illustrate this fact and in particular to show the kind of influence which worship had at that earliest stage upon the development of doctrine.

In the study of the Pastoral epistles it has frequently been pointed out that the most obviously 'Pauline' elements there are to be found in the 'faithful sayings' or other phrases of a similarly stylized kind. A striking example is the saying of 2 Tim. ii. 11–12, 'Faithful is the saying: For if we died with him, we shall also live with him; if we endure, we shall also reign with him.' The balanced form of these words has led the great majority of commentators to assume that they are a quotation from a baptismal hymn. The assumption would seem well grounded. But it is also evident that the words convey very effectively the Pauline doctrine of baptism as death and resurrection with Christ, a doctrine which would seem to be a long way away from the characteristic ideas of the author of the epistle. It would therefore appear that liturgical practice has here provided the effective medium for conserving and transmitting to the next generation an important doctrinal concept.

My second example is of a much more fundamental and far-reaching kind. In the closing verses
of 1 Corinthians, Paul includes the famous Aramaic
phrase, 'Maranatha', 'Lord, come'. The words
are most naturally understood as an invocation in
prayer to Jesus as Lord. It has often been pointed
out that the Aramaic form of the phrase strongly
suggests that such practice goes back to a very
early stage in the life of the Church, to a time before
the development of the Gentile Greek-speaking
churches. But the passage is almost equally
significant as evidence of the important role played
by worship in the development of Christological
ideas. Jesus was clearly invoked in worship from
the very start of the Church's life, and he was
invoked under the title 'Lord', the most natural
form of address in prayer or worship. But the
Greek word for Lord (κύριος) embodies in itself
a remarkable weight of meaning. It is the regular
translation of the divine name in the Old Testament, and Phil. ii. 5–11 (another possibly liturgical
passage) suggests that to call Jesus 'Lord' is to
give him that divine name whose glory Yahweh
had declared should not be shared with any other.
Thus it was a title given to him in worship and
continually used of him in that context which
helped to give expression to some of the highest
Christological affirmations in the whole of the New
Testament.

64

In these examples can be seen two ways in which worship had an influence at a very early stage on the development of doctrine. On the one hand, it exercised a conservative function; it proved an effective medium for giving memorable expression to the ideas of one place or one generation and transmitting them to other people and subsequent generations. At the same time, it could also play a more creative role. The continuing practice of invoking the name of Jesus in worship helped to ensure that when the time came for more precise doctrinal definition of his person it would be in terms which did not fall short of the manner of his address in worship. In both these ways the practice of worship continued to influence the development of doctrine in the succeeding centuries.

Our knowledge of the Church's worship in the second and third centuries is based on very fragmentary evidence. But one feature stands out at a glance. The more formal prayers of the Church's liturgy were prayers offered to God through Jesus Christ. For this fact there are many witnesses. The first eucharistic thanksgiving of that strange but almost certainly very early work known as the *Didache* or *Teaching of the Twelve Apostles* is addressed to the Father and ends with the words 'for thine is the glory and the power through Jesus Christ for ever and ever'.[1] Justin

---

[1] *Didache*, 9.

Martyr, who provides us with our earliest descriptive account of a eucharistic service, describes the prayers and thanksgivings of that service as an offering of 'praise and glory to the Father of the universe through the name of the Son and of the Holy Ghost'.[1] This evidence finds further support in the earliest surviving service books, which are of a slightly later date. The prayers to be found in the *Apostolic Tradition* of Hippolytus, which comes from Rome in the early years of the third century, and in the *Euchologion* (or Prayer-book) of Serapion, which comes from Egypt in the middle of the fourth, both reveal the same pattern of liturgical prayer.

But this rule did not apply to the more popular forms of piety. In the New Testament itself the dying Stephen calls directly upon the Lord Jesus, and the new song of the four-and-twenty elders in Rev. v is a hymn of praise addressed to the Lamb. In both these spheres, brief ejaculatory prayer and hymnody, a direct address to Christ remained the custom of the second and third centuries. The majority of martyrs are recorded to have followed Stephen in calling directly upon Jesus.[2] Pliny describes the Christians in Bithynia as meeting to sing a hymn to Christ as a God. By itself Pliny's

[1] *Apol.* 1. 65. Cf. also 1. 67.
[2] See the collection of prayers of the martyrs in A. Hamman, *Early Christian Prayers* (E.T.) (1961), pp. 50–60. Even if not all the recorded prayers are based on reliable testimony, there can be no doubting the genuineness of the tenor of the prayers, particularly in the case of the ordinary Christians of no special rank or fame.

testimony would be too indirect for us to be able to place any reliance upon it, but it is borne out by the scanty evidence of such early hymnody as has come down to us. The *Phōs Hilaron* is an early evening hymn which probably goes back to the second century and which is still used today in the Church's worship. Its opening words are familiar to many in the translation of John Keble: 'Hail gladdening light, of his pure glory poured who is the immortal Father, heavenly, blest, holiest of holies, Jesus Christ our Lord.' The address here is directly to Christ. The same is true of the hymn, probably composed by Clement himself, which stands at the very end of his work, the *Paidagogos*, where Christ is praised as:

> King of Saints, almighty Word
> Of the Father, highest Lord;
> Wisdom's head and chief;
> Assuagement of all grief;
> Lord of all time and space,
> Jesus, Saviour of our race.[1]

This popular piety, in both its forms of informal prayers addressed to the Son and hymnody, seems to have been most common in circles associated with Gnostic teaching. In the Apocryphal Acts Christ is frequently addressed by such a title as

[1] Translation from the Ante-Nicene Fathers, *Clement of Alexandria*, I, 343.

5-2

'God most high' (θέε ὕψιστε),[1] and Hippolytus records of one particular Gnostic sect, the Naasenes, that they had composed many and various hymns to the archetypal man whom they called Adam.[2] It is not surprising that Gnostic piety should have taken such forms. The Gnostic Christ was a denizen exclusively of the spiritual world and more naturally, therefore, one to whom prayer was to be addressed. Moreover, effective hymnody requires a measure of free play on the part of the poetic imagination which came more naturally to the Gnostic mind. Clement's hymn with its wide-ranging imagery is perhaps a characteristic example of the way in which he takes over and baptizes into orthodox Christianity ways of thought and expression whose natural home was in Gnosticism.

This popular piety had a considerable influence on the developing theology of the Church. Christians worshipped the Son. Theologians, like Justin Martyr, had no hesitation in acknowledging that fact and the propriety of it, however difficult they might find it to explain to their pagan critics.[3] But explanation there had to be. Christians in the second century were obviously liable to the charge of having abandoned monotheism. Did they not admit to the worship of God the Father and of

---

[1] E.g. Acts of Peter 39 (ed. Bonnet, p. 96; another example of a martyr's prayer); Acts of Thomas 47, 48, 60, 107 (ed. Bonnet, pp. 164, 164, 177, 219); Acts of John 108–15 (ed. Bonnet, pp. 207, 208, 212, 213, 215).
[2] Hippolytus, *Haer.* 5. 6. 5.   [3] *Apol.* 1. 13; *Dial.* 68.

Christ? And was not this tantamount to admitting two divinities? Those whose approach to theology was dominated by a determination to rebut such a charge at all costs have usually been known as Monarchians, men who were determined to uphold the monarchy or single rule of God. The only clearcut and unequivocal way in which this could be done was by denying either the divinity of Christ or the distinction between him and God the Father. On many counts those who followed the first line of denying the divinity of Christ—usually known as Dynamic Monarchians because they regarded Christ as a man endowed with a special *dunamis* or power by God—might have seemed to have the stronger case. If it was a matter of appeal to Scripture, there was more surface evidence there to suggest a radical difference between Father and Son than to suggest their identity. Biblical exegesis of this kind, with special reference to the Synoptic Gospels, was certainly an important aspect of the arguments used by Theodotus of Byzantium, one of the earliest exponents of this type of thought. Similarly, if it was a matter of appeal to tradition, the Dynamic Monarchians again had a strong case. Artemon is reported to have claimed that his teaching represented the original apostolic tradition. Christ, he claimed, had not been regarded as God by the church of Rome before the time of Pope Victor in the closing years of the second century. That claim, if it be restricted to the sphere of explicit theological statement, is not far from the truth. Yet despite this measure of justifiable appeal to Scripture and to theological tradition, Dynamic Monarchianism not only failed to win the day; it was never even in the race. It could not give any adequate explanation of the Church's worship of Christ and so it had no chance of acceptance as the Church's theology. Eusebius records that Artemon's claim to be continuing traditional teaching was answered explicitly at the time by appeal to the Church's established practice of singing hymns to Christ. His theology, it was claimed, could not be squared with 'all the psalms or songs written from the beginning by faithful brethren, which celebrate the Word of God, even Christ, and speak of him as God'.[1] The ablest exponent of this approach was Paul of Samosata, who was deposed from his bishopric for heresy in A.D. 268. It is interesting to note that he is recorded to have 'put a stop to psalms addressed to our Lord Jesus Christ on the ground that they are modern and the compositions of modern men'. His detractors claimed that it was because he preferred to have psalms addressed to himself; no doubt the real reason was that such psalms gave effective expression to that popular piety which was the real stumbling-block to any acceptance of his theological views.[2]

[1] Eusebius, *H.E.* 5. 28. 5.   [2] *Ibid.* 7. 30. 10.

It was here that the other kind of Monarchian—
usually called Modalist Monarchian because he
denied any real distinction between the Father and
the Son and regarded the Son simply as an alternative mode of the Father's being—was able to make
so much greater an appeal. His case might involve
difficult exegesis of some parts of Scripture—but
some parts of Scripture were clearly in need of
subtle exegesis; it might involve more advanced
views than those previously expressed by theologians—but it could be presented as simply
making more explicit what was the implication of
those earlier views. Were not the worship and
glorification of Christ the heart of the Church's
piety? And did not Modalist Monarchianism give
the fullest possible expression to that exalted task?
It is not difficult to catch the tones of aggrieved
surprise in Noetus' reply to the presbytery which
examined his teaching when he declared, 'Why,
what evil am I doing in glorifying Christ?'[1] The
thorough-going modalism of Noetus could not
itself become the accepted teaching of the main
body of the Church. It rode roughshod over too
much of the evidence. But it had an obvious and
immediate appeal because it seemed to do fullest
justice to the popular conception of piety. And
for that same reason the final teaching of the
Church about the person of the Son bears a greater

[1] Hippolytus, *Contra Noetum*, 1.

resemblance to that of Noetus than to that of Theodotus.

But the dominating influence of the early third century was the person of Origen and the basic pattern of his thought was strongly opposed to modalist teaching. The fact of the three distinct persons of the godhead was for him a fundamental datum of all theological thinking. Origen was a Christian thinker whose basic currency was a currency of ideas, but he was also a man of prayer and of the Church. His teaching about the person of the Son was not determined exclusively on grounds of philosophical speculation. It also took serious account of the role of the Son in the prayer life of the Christian and in the worshipping life of the Church.

Origen readily admits that Scripture includes prayers to Christ and that it is the practice of Christians to sing hymns to Christ as well as to the supreme God.[1] But he draws a distinction between these prayers and hymns and those offered to God himself. Jesus, he points out, instructs us to offer our prayers to the Father in his name.[2] This is therefore the proper pattern for Christian prayer. Prayer in the fullest sense of the word (κυριολεξία) should not be offered to Christ but only to the Father through him. Prayer offered to Christ is prayer only in a secondary sense of that word (καταχρηστικῶς), for strictly understood it is a

[1] *De Or.* 14.6 (Stephen); *Con. Cel.* 8.67.   [2] *De Or.* 15.2.

request to the Logos as high priest of all the angelic host to convey our prayers to the Father's throne of grace.[1] He himself had no hesitation in using informal, ejaculatory prayers to the Son. Many examples are to be found in the *Homilies*.[2] Moreover, his *Commentary on the Song of Songs* did much to enhance this form of devotion. Presumably (though he is not explicit on this point) he expected to see what he regarded as the theologically correct pattern of praying carefully observed in the more formal liturgical prayers of the Church. The evidence which we have considered so far strongly suggests that contemporary practice did in fact follow very much the lines which Origen would have desired. It is true that he does complain of a dangerous division between those who pray to the Father and those who pray to the Son.[3] Presumably his complaint is not simply that praying to the Son exists, for as we have seen he himself practises a form of such prayer, but rather that it has such a hold on some people that they have wrongly come to regard it as the normative pattern of true prayer.

This distinction between two kinds of prayer, absolute and relative (κυρίως and καταχρηστικῶς), corresponds precisely to the theological distinction

[1] *De Or.* 15.1; *Con. Cel.* 5.4, 8.13, 8.26.
[2] For a representative selection of examples, see C. Bigg, *Christian Platonists of Alexandria* (2nd edn, 1913), pp. 228-9, n. 1.
[3] *De Or.* 16.1.

which Origen draws between the Father and the Son. The Father alone is God in the fullest sense of the word and has the attributes of deity in that fullest sense; the Son has his deity and the proper attributes of deity in a lesser sense (κατα-χρηστικῶς). No doubt this distinction was evolved by Origen primarily for theological reasons as a part of his interpretation of Christianity in terms of that hierarchical view of godhead which he shared with Middle Platonism. But its application to the sphere of prayer and worship was no mere afterthought. Any interpretation of the person of the Son had to be one which came to terms with the place given to him in the Christian practice of devotion. In so far as it was a question of coming to terms with prayer and worship as described in the New Testament, Origen's case was a strong one. Indeed on that score alone, it is those who would reject the kind of distinction which Origen draws upon whom the burden of proof lies. But Origen's theology did involve saying that the popular piety of his day (in which he himself was fully prepared to participate) should not be regarded as doctrinally normative. There need have been nothing sur-prising in that. It is the official liturgy of the Church rather than popular piety which one might presume to be more suited to act as a guide to theological understanding. Nevertheless, in the long run the popular piety of devotion to the person

74

of Jesus was not content to be taken with anything less than full theological seriousness. Worship of Christ and prayer to him were too firmly entrenched in the ground-soil of the life of the Church to be treated as deviations (even fully permissible deviations) from the exact canons of theological rectitude.

So when Athanasius insists, as he does, that the heart of Arian error is that it would make Christians guilty of worshipping a creature,[1] he is speaking not so much as an interpreter of the Church's liturgy but rather as a defender 'of the "simple faith" of the Church'.[2] Indeed it was the opponents of the new orthodoxy who could (and did) most easily appeal to the precise structure of the Church's liturgy as lending support for their views.[3] But once the doctrinal issue about the person of the Son had been brought so decisively into the open with the Arian controversy, the interaction of doctrine and liturgy on that issue becomes one of doctrine consciously influencing liturgy, rather than the other way around. This

[1] E.g. *Ad Adelphium*, 3–4.
[2] Cf. T. E. Pollard, 'Logos and Son in Origen, Arius and Athanasius', *Studia Patristica* II, Texte und Untersuchungen 9 (1957), p. 287.
[3] See G. Mercati, *Antiche Relique Liturgiche* (Studi e Testi, 7) (1902), pp. 51–3. There is no satisfactory terminology for referring to those whom I have here described as 'opponents of the new orthodoxy'. 'Arian' is too strong a term; many of them explicitly disclaim the title, and much of the thought most distinctive of Arius is missing. 'Eastern conservative' or 'subordinationist' is a better term, but should not be allowed to suggest that they were simply living in the past; they were thoughtfully working out their position in terms of the fourth-century post-Arius situation.

THE MAKING OF CHRISTIAN DOCTRINE

influence operated in both Arian and orthodox circles. The text of the *Gloria in Excelsis*, as we now have it, is a song of praise addressed initially and primarily to the Father but passing somewhat awkwardly into prayer addressed to the Son.[1] This seems to be the outcome of a conflation of two versions. It started as one of the ante-Nicene hymns to Christ. The Arianizing or strongly conservative author of the *Apostolic Constitutions* transformed it into a hymn addressed exclusively to the Father, and this version has left its mark on the version now used by us.[2] But the modifications

[1] 'Glory be to God on high, and on earth peace, good will towards men. We praise thee, we bless thee, we worship thee, we glorify thee, we give thanks to thee for thy great glory, O Lord God, heavenly King, God the Father Almighty. O Lord, the only begotten Son Jesus Christ; O Lord God, Lamb of God, Son of the Father, that takest away the sins of the world, have mercy upon us . . .' There is nothing strange in a hymn being addressed in its opening section to the Father and then in a later part to the Son, but the lack of symmetry in the two forms of address does make the transition in this case a rather clumsy one.

[2] For a full discussion of the evidence see B. Capelle, 'Le Texte du "Gloria in Excelsis"', *R.H.E.* XLIV (1949), 439–57. A strong case has been made for identifying Ps.-Ignatius (and consequently the author of the Apostolic Constitutions) as Eusebius of Emesa (O. Perler, 'Pseudo-Ignatius und Eusebius von Emesa', *Historisches Jahrbuch*, LXXVII, 1958, 77–82). One of the characteristics of this otherwise Arianizing author is his insistence on the impassibility of the Son (cf. Theodoret, *Eranistes Dial.* III–*P.G.* 83, 312 b). Capelle points out that this feature also appears in one of Mai's fragments of Arian Sermons (*P.L.* 13, 605). The liturgical argument for Arianism, or at least subordinationism, which we have already quoted from Mercati's edition of some of the fragments, belongs to the same collection (*P.L.* 13, 611–12). This suggests a common school of thought with strong liturgical interests, in which Eusebius of Emesa may have been a particularly significant figure. For similar alterations by the author of the Constitutions to the text before him, cf. *Ap. Con.* 5. 6; 6.14 and 6.30 with *Didascalia*, 5. 6; 6. 12 and 6. 23 respectively.

76

which have left their mark were, naturally enough, for the most part those made in an orthodox direction. The exaltation of the Son in orthodox teaching led to the development of liturgical prayers being addressed directly to him, a practice apparently unknown before. It is just possible that some liturgies of this kind are a direct development of earlier popular semi-Gnostic usage, but the main cause was undoubtedly the influence of the new doctrinal ideas.[1] In the West, liturgical developments of this kind are to be found primarily in Gaul and Spain at a time when the Catholic church was very conscious of standing over against the Arianism of her Gothic overlords. But it was in the Eastern church with its more pluralistic approach to the godhead that the development took more lasting root.

But these developments lie outside our present concern, which is the influence of the practice of worship on the early, creative stages of doctrinal development. We have been concerned so far with its influence on the development of belief with regard to the second person of the Trinity. If we move on to consider development of belief in the third person, the vital role played by the worshipping life of the Church is once again clearly evident.

[1] Acts of Thomas 49 (ed. Bonnet, p. 166) and Acts of John 109 (ed. Bonnet, p. 207) are examples of eucharistic prayers addressed to Jesus in popular Gnosticizing writings. Cf. E. C. Ratcliff, 'The Original Form of the Anaphora of Addai and Mari', *J.T.S.* xxx (1928), 23 ff.

In the case of the Holy Spirit there is even less in the text of the New Testament to compel belief in a third, co-equal person of the godhead. It is true that there are passages in which he is conjoined in some kind of threefold formula with the Father and the Son. But there are other texts which would suggest a less exalted, even a less personal, status for the Holy Spirit. Indeed the paucity of scriptural evidence was something of an embarrassment to the Church's theologians when they sought to demonstrate the Spirit's full divinity in the closing years of the fourth century. Gregory of Nazianzus was forced to develop a special doctrine of development to meet the point. He does not, of course, admit that Scripture does not indicate the divinity of the Spirit at all, but he does admit that it does not make the point explicit. This he explains as part of a pattern of development. The Old Testament had proclaimed the Father openly, the Son more obscurely; the New showed the divinity of the Son clearly and suggested that of the Spirit. Finally, in the life of the Church, the Spirit was present and was supplying a clear demonstration of his true nature.[1] Gregory's argument is one of unusual interest, but it is perhaps developed a little too obviously to meet the difficulty in hand. Basil of Caesarea also is embarrassed by the lack of direct scriptural evidence for the divinity of the

[1] *Or.* 31. 26.

Spirit. The best he can do is to quote three passages in which the title Lord is apparently ascribed to the Holy Spirit. He quotes 2 Thess. iii. 15, 'May the Lord direct your hearts to the love of God and to the steadfastness of Christ,' where he argues that the first 'Lord' must refer to the Holy Spirit in view of the explicit reference to the other two persons later in the same sentence, a similar phrase from 1 Thess. iii. 12–13, and finally the more obvious words from 2 Cor. iii. 17, 'The Lord is the Spirit'.[1] The last of these three citations sounds rather more impressive when quoted in isolation than when studied in its original context, but even apart from any such consideration it is clear that Basil's case when viewed as an argument from Scripture is not a strong one.

If, then, the case for the full divinity of the Spirit is so difficult to establish on scriptural grounds alone, how did it come to be the accepted doctrine of the Church? One factor of vital importance, particularly in the early stages, was the fact that baptism was regularly administered in the threefold name of Father, Son and Holy Spirit. Second-century writers show comparatively little interest in the Spirit. As long as their thought about the second person was primarily in terms of the Logos, there was little incentive, as far as the requirements of their own theological thinking were concerned,

[1] *De Spir. San.* 52.

to develop any detailed doctrine of the Holy Spirit. Those aspects of God's working within the natural processes of the world or within human experience which might most readily have prompted deeper reflexion about the nature and the working of the Holy Spirit were for them most naturally understood in relation to the Logos. Where more definite mention of the Spirit does occur, it is very frequently to be found in an explicitly baptismal context.[1]

In the early years of the third century, as thought about the second person began to centre more upon the idea of Son than of Logos, interest in the person and work of the Holy Spirit increased. But it is still in baptismal contexts that much of the most significant teaching is to be found. In his attack on modalism, for example, Tertullian cites the practice of triple immersion at the mention of each of the three names prescribed in the Lord's command to baptize 'in the name of the Father and of the Son and of the Holy Ghost' (Matt. xxvii. 19) as evidence for faith in the three distinct persons of the godhead.[2]

Thus in the dormant years when little theological interest was shown in the person of the Spirit, it was the continuing fact of baptismal practice which did most to keep alive the idea of the Holy Spirit as a third alongside the Father and the Son. In the early years of the third century, as conscious interest in the Spirit began to grow, baptismal

[1] E.g. Justin, *Apol.* 1.13.   [2] *Adv. Prax.* 26.

practice was appealed to as evidence of the divine and distinct nature of the Spirit. And finally in the fourth century, when the stage of more formal definition of the doctrine was reached, the same ground of appeal recurs. Athanasius argues in his letters to Serapion that since the name of the Holy Spirit is solemnly conjoined with those of the Father and the Son in the most fundamental experience of baptism, they cannot be fundamentally disparate in nature.[1] Basil, similarly, in setting out his beliefs about the Spirit, cites the practice of baptism as the first and basic evidence for his positive convictions.[2]

Indeed the whole context of debate which gave rise to Basil's famous treatise on the Holy Spirit was a context of worship, not indeed of baptismal practice but of the correct form of doxology. For the use of the threefold doxology is a second context in the sphere of liturgical practice of great significance for the doctrine of the Spirit. Basil tells us in the *De Spiritu Sancto* that he himself used two different forms, giving glory to God the Father either *through* the Son *in* the Holy Spirit or *with* (μετά) the Son *together with* (σύν) the Holy Spirit (3). He regarded both as proper forms, the former more appropriate to a context of thanksgiving for God's gifts, the latter in adoration (16). His opponents objected to the latter form and regarded it as an undesirable innovation. There is

---

[1] *Ep. ad Ser.* 1. 29-30.   [2] *De Spir. San.* 24 ff.

no doubt that threefold doxologies go back to an early date, but, as Basil recognized, the possibility of alterations to the brief but crucial prepositional words in the course of copying and handing down the early texts makes determination of their precise form at the earliest stage difficult to achieve with any confidence. He himself quotes the support of Clement of Rome, Irenaeus, Origen, Julius Africanus, Dionysius of Rome, Dionysius of Alexandria, Gregory Thaumaturgus and Eusebius of Caesarea (72–4). Not all Basil's citations are to the point, and the issue is best investigated independently of his assertions.

Justin Martyr is our earliest (though indirect) witness to the use of the threefold doxology in worship, but it is in a form stressing the mediatorial role of the Son and of the Spirit, using the preposition 'through' in each case.[1] The earliest example of a doxology using the preposition 'with' of both Son and Spirit is the account of the Martyrdom of Polycarp. We have already seen that the martyrdom records are a context in which prayer to Jesus is prominent. It is therefore a not unlikely context for the first appearance of this more co-ordinated doxological form. Nevertheless, there is ground for doubt about the reliability of the text and it is impossible to form any confident

[1] *Apol.* 1. 65, 67. Cf. p. 66 above. On the early doxologies, see especially J. Lebreton, *Histoire du Dogme de la Trinité* (1927), II, note A, 'Les Doxologies', pp. 618–30.

judgement about its original form.[1] Clement of
Alexandria's prayer to the Word of God as man's
Instructor or *Paidagogos* at the close of the work
that bears that name gives praise and thanks to
the Father and the Son with the Holy Spirit;[2]
but the prayer is of an informal, poetic nature, and
in the more formal doxology which closes his
homily on Mark x. 17-31, entitled 'Who is the
Rich Man that is saved?', he uses the preposition
'through', stressing the mediatorial role of Son and
Spirit alike. Most of the homilies of Origen close
with a doxology of some kind, but trinitarian forms
occur only in homilies available to us in Latin
translation, where no confidence can be placed on
the precise wording employed; the doxology with
which the treatise on prayer closes is, as we might
expect in the light of the interpretation of prayer
given in that work itself, one offered to the Father
of all through Jesus Christ in the Holy Spirit.

The author who, in the light of the texts available to us, offers the best support for Basil's cause
is one whom he does not cite and who on general
theological grounds might antecedently be thought
a most unlikely source—namely, Hippolytus. Hippolytus' treatise, the *Apostolic Tradition*, is the
earliest substantial work of a liturgical nature
which we have. It is therefore particularly apposite

---

[1] *Martyrdom of Polycarp*, 14. Cf. J. A. Robinson, 'The Doxology in
the Prayer of St Polycarp', *J.T.S.* XXIV (1923), 141-4.
[2] *Paid.* 3. 101. 2.

to the present discussion. In view of the textual difficulties with which any study of it is involved, we might anticipate that it would be peculiarly difficult to determine the precise form of doxology which it prescribes; but in fact we are able to reach a very high degree of confidence in this case. Hippolytus lays down that every blessing should take the form 'To thee be glory, to the Father and to the Son with (?the) Holy Spirit in the holy church now and for ever and world without end'. Precisely the same form stands at the close of another work of Hippolytus, the *Contra Noetum*. The process of attaching this doxology to the various prayers of the *Apostolic Tradition* tends to produce the rather cumbersome form 'through whom (i.e. Christ) to thee with him and with the Holy Spirit...'[1] But this does nothing to alter the basic fact that with Hippolytus we have a doxology offered to the Father with the Son and with the Holy Spirit. Moreover, the *Apostolic Tradition* is a text which had great influence on later liturgies.

The form of doxology most familiar to us, 'Glory be to the Father and to the Son and to the Holy Ghost', co-ordinates the three persons more closely still by using 'and' rather than 'with' to join the three names. There is good reason for believing that this form was an innovation during the troubled times of the Antiochene schism in the

---

[1] See R. H. Connolly, *J.T.S.* XXIV (1923), 144–6.

middle of the fourth century. The form of Gloria used was regarded as a way of expressing one's partisan loyalty. Leontius, the cautious bishop who stood for a policy of the greatest degree of comprehension in the church, was forced to indulge in the subterfuge of reciting the doxology so inaudibly that only its closing words, 'world without end', could be heard distinctly.[1] Two sources describe the ultra-orthodox Flavian as responsible for introducing the form with two *and*s at this time with set theological intent.[2] As Fr. Thurston has written: 'All things considered it does certainly seem to be a fact that the existing version of our little prayer (that with two *and*s), itself obviously based upon the formula of baptism, was originally introduced at Antioch in the fourth century with the distinct purpose of emphasizing the true Trinitarian doctrine and of counteracting the dangerous leaven of Arianism.'[3] In the case of this particular form of the Gloria, therefore, we can be pretty confident that it was a product rather than a cause of doctrinal conviction about the co-equality of the persons of the Trinity.

This discussion of the early forms of doxology and their relation to the developing doctrine of the

[1] Theodoret, *H.E.* 2. 19.
[2] Philostorgius, *H.E.* 3. 13; Nicetas, *Thesaurus* 5. 30 (*P.G.* 139, 1390). Nicetas, though writing as late as the thirteenth century, explicitly quotes the authority of Theodore of Mopsuestia for his assertion.
[3] H. Thurston, 'The "Gloria Patri"', *The Month*, CXXXI (1918), 412.

Spirit cannot be expected in the nature of the evidence to lead to any clear or decisive conclusions. We cannot doubt that the use from an early date of doxologies which mention the three persons of the godhead did much to further the sense of the Spirit's divinity in the mind of the Church. But as with the practice of liturgical prayer through Christ, those doxologies were normally expressed in a form which was as compatible with a view which ascribes a radically subordinate position to the second and third persons of the Trinity as it was with later orthodoxy. The most surprising feature of all is the fact that the early writer who most clearly speaks of the Spirit as co-recipient and not merely the medium of the offering of praise is Hippolytus, who, when speaking theologically, is hesitant even to call the Spirit a third person (πρόσωπον) alongside the two persons of Father and Son. The practice of threefold doxologies was no doubt influential, but their form was equivocal. When they do appear in doctrinally unequivocal form, it is because they have been explicitly so designed in a doctrinally self-conscious age. Behind that most unequivocal form lies, no doubt, as Thurston suggests, the baptismal formula. And when the other forms are interpreted as implying a fully co-equal Trinity, it is because they are consciously interpreted in the light of that formula.[1]

---

[1] Basil, *De Spir. San.* 59.

It is therefore to the baptismal formula that we are continually driven back as the supremely significant influence in the development of the doctrine of the Spirit.

The interrelation of worship and doctrine in the early centuries is a subject of far broader scope than can be dealt with in a single chapter. Nothing has been said here about the influence of liturgical practice on the doctrine of the sacraments. The likelihood, indeed the inevitability, of such influence is obvious enough, though the detail is often difficult to trace with any confidence. The traffic of such influence was a two-way traffic and it is not always easy to be sure which way the movement has taken place. There is room here for much detailed study and continuing research. But my concern has been limited to the influence of worship at the central point of Christian doctrine, belief about the nature of God and of the divine Trinity. There can be no questioning the importance of that influence. If the issues at stake had been matter for intellectual argument alone, the pattern of development would have been very different. Whatever the intellectual merits of Dynamic Monarchianism, Origenist subordinationism and philosophical Arianism, they failed very largely because they did not do justice to Christian apprehension of the Son as a fitting object of worship and adoration. The full divinity of the

Holy Spirit could still be doubted more than three and a half centuries after Pentecost, but no one factor was of greater importance for the settlement of the issue than the long-hallowed institution of triple immersion into the threefold name at baptism.

That has often been said before, and I believe it to be true. But something more needs to be said if not only the strength but also the possible weakness in this facet of early development is to be faced. The instinct of worship which helped Athanasius to triumph over Arius was not the pattern of ordered liturgical development but the pattern of popular devotion. Origen's account in the *De Oratione* of two kinds of praying is normally dismissed as a forced but unsuccessful attempt to fit the worshipping life of the Church into the narrow confines of his alien intellectual system. Indeed it is usually argued that he does not himself live by his own rule and that he is nearer to the truth in his practice than in his theorizing.[1] But need Origen be so interpreted? Cannot his account be seen as one which does justice alike to the more accurate formularies of the liturgy and the freer rein of private devotion? Origen's theory is not incompatible with his practice, though it represents a more sophisticated account of that devotional practice than

[1] See especially J. Lebreton, 'Le Désaccord de la foi populaire et de la théologie savante dans l'église chrétienne du IIIe siècle', *R.H.E.* XIX (1923), 481–506; XX (1924), 5–37.

the ordinary believer might be anxious to accept. If, then, the worshipping instinct which was of primary influence in the earliest development of Christian doctrine was that of untutored popular devotion, we must pause before we accept its validity uncritically.

There is one area of doctrine in Christian history where development is unquestionably due to the successful influence of popular devotion—the sphere of Mariological doctrine. This is freely admitted by those alike who would approve and disapprove that development. A Roman Catholic scholar writes: 'C'est merveille que l'idée ait fait son chemin malgré tout, ait conquis les Docteurs, soit devenue la foi explicite de l'Eglise; c'est un des cas les plus beaux et les plus touchants de la piété, je ne dis pas . . . triomphant de la science, mais devançant la science, stimulant la science à ratifier les intuitions de l'amour et de la piété.'[1] A Protestant scholar writes: 'Those who know the history of Mariology . . . know how the weighty theologians stood shoulder to shoulder against its uncontrolled growth, but how the pious monks and the simple devotion of the people kept pushing along the glorification uncontrollably until today we have, even officially, the doctrine of the Bodily Assumption.'[2] The value judgements of the

[1] J. V. Bainvel, 'L'Histoire d'un dogme', *Etudes*, CI (1914), 617, 620-1, 623-5, quoted by H. de Lubac, 'Le Problème du développement du dogme', *R.S.R.* XXXV (1948), 134.
[2] N. F. S. Ferré, *Christ and the Christian* (1958), p. 31.

two statements differ; their reading of the central facts of the case is the same.

I do not wish to suggest that all popular devotion is of the same (negligible) value as evidence or to imply that these two examples of popular devotion are of just the same kind. But the parallel at least forces us to recognize that popular devotion is no infallible guide. We must be ready to admit that the popular devotion of the ante-Nicene period may have been more powerful as a historical and psychological force leading to the triumph of orthodoxy than it is as a rational ground of appeal for the truth of that doctrine today. It may still serve as one link in the chain of evidence, but there are limits to the weight that it can bear by itself.

The other, more liturgical feature of early worship which has emerged as a particularly potent force in influencing doctrinal development is the use of the threefold name in baptism. Here again we need to ask if its true nature is such as to justify the great influence which undoubtedly it had. Matt. xxviii. 19 describes the risen Christ as instructing his disciples to 'teach all nations, baptizing them in the name of the Father and of the Son and of the Holy Ghost'. The question whether this saying ought to be regarded as an actual utterance of Christ himself has been frequently and extensively debated. But that is not the significant issue. The vital issue is the question how much was implied by the close conjoining of the three names at whatever time or place it came first to be practised. Those who have argued that there are no valid historical or theological grounds for denying its authenticity as a dominical saying have cited the implicitly 'trinitarian' form suggested by such texts as 1 Cor. vi. 11, 'In the name of the Lord Jesus Christ and in (ἐν) the Spirit of our God.'[1] But the argument can be used in a different way. If it is evidence that the conjoining of the three names in a baptismal context belongs to the earliest stage of New Testament tradition, it is also evidence that that conjunction was possible without implying identity of role or status to the three persons named. Clearly this is not implied by the form of reference in 1 Corinthians. The fact that in Matt. xxviii. 19 the three names are brought so much more closely together under the common heading 'in the name of' *could* imply that the three names are there regarded as referring to differing persons of the co-equal godhead; it *need* not imply so much. Strack–Billerbeck indicate the generality of meaning borne by the term 'in the name of' in Semitic usage, and even quote one example where six disparate entities are joined by that common phrase.[2] By itself the phrase to

[1] E.g. R. E. O. White, *The Biblical Doctrine of Initiation* (1960), p. 341.
[2] Strack–Billerbeck, *Kommentar zum Neuen Testament*, vol. 1 (1922), p. 1055 (quoted by G. R. Beasley-Murray, *Baptism in the New Testament* (1962), p. 91).

baptize 'in the name of the Father and of the Son and of the Holy Ghost' could well be an expansion of a primitive baptism 'in the name of Christ' which meant no more than baptism 'in the name of Christ who was sent by God and who himself baptizes with the Holy Spirit now being poured out upon all flesh'.[1] A. C. McGiffert has suggested that there may well have been an intermediate stage between the two in which baptism was in the name of God, Jesus Christ and the Holy Spirit. This is the commonest form of triadic collocation in the earliest strand of Christian literature. In particular, a version of it is twice used in the account of baptism given by Justin where new converts are described as 'receiving the washing with water in the name of God, the Father and Lord of the universe, and of our Saviour Jesus Christ, and of the Holy Spirit'.[2] It ought not, McGiffert claims, to be treated as if it were just the same as the form 'Father, Son and Holy Spirit'.[3] Is the author of the *Apostolic Constitutions*, whom we have already seen to be a key figure in a sub-ordinationist interpretation of the liturgy, being guilty of special pleading when he paraphrases Matt. xxviii. 19 as a command 'to preach the gospel to all the world, and to make disciples of

[1] Cf. M. Barth, *Die Taufe—ein Sakrament?* (1951), p. 552.
[2] *Apol.* 1. 61.
[3] A. C. McGiffert, *The Apostles' Creed* (1902), pp. 181–2.

all nations, and to baptize them into his death by
the authority of the God of the universe who is his
Father and by the testimony of the Spirit who is
his Paraclete'?[1]

Legem credendi lex statuat supplicandi. When first
used, those words had a specific reference. They
were an appeal to the implications of the particular
injunctions about prayer set out in I Timothy ii. I
with reference to the Pelagian controversy. In the
course of history they have often been quoted with
a very much wider reference. Undoubtedly the
practice of prayer has had its effect on doctrine;
undoubtedly the practice of prayer *should* have its
effect on doctrine. But that is not to say that the
effect which prayer has actually had is at every
point precisely the effect which it should have had.

[1] *Ap. Const.* 5.7. (Cf. also *ibid.* 3.17.) The Clementine Homilies
similarly combine baptism in the threefold name (9.23; 11.26) with a
clear denial that the Son is God from God (16.15). They do also include
a doxology to Father and Son and Holy Spirit, but this is most likely
to be a later addition (3.72).

5

SOTERIOLOGY

THE last chapter was concerned with the influence exercised by the worshipping life of the Church on the development of doctrine. The Church's doctrines of Christ and of the Holy Spirit had to keep pace with the role ascribed to them in prayer and worship. Prayer and worship take many different forms. At their purest and highest they are concerned simply with the adoration of God in himself. It was for such worship that Basil argued the propriety of using a doxology in which the three persons of the Trinity are co-ordinated in equal balance. But worship is not always or all the time so disinterested a process.

In prayer man asks. He asks (if he is obedient to the famous saying which, though appearing in no known gospel, is ascribed by Clement of Alexandria and others to Jesus) 'for the great things', the things most needful for his spiritual well-being.[1] In worship, especially in sacramental worship, he expects to receive those things for which he asks, the things which go to make up his salvation. Certainly Christian faith was never

[1] 'Ask ye for the great things and God will add unto you the little things' (see J. Jeremias, *Unknown Sayings of Jesus* (2nd edn, 1964), pp. 98–100).

presented as nothing more than information about the true way of worshipping God. It was that but, because it was that, it was also and emphatically a way of salvation. If popular piety was determined at every point to insist that doctrinal affirmations must be such as would do justice to Christianity as a way of worship, it was still more determined that they should also do justice to Christianity as a way of salvation. Even in the most technically philosophical and dogmatic debates, issues of soteriological concern were always of paramount importance.

Now, the underlying conviction of the genuinely religious man about salvation is that its source can only be God himself. This fundamental axiom was a basic criterion of orthodox thought in all the great fourth- and fifth-century controversies. In particular it was a decisive factor in the victory of Athanasius over Arius.

Arian doctrine has been described by Gwatkin as 'a mass of presumptuous theorizing, supported by alternate scraps of obsolete traditionalism and uncritical text-mongering',[1] which is another way of saying that it is based on reason, tradition and Scripture and that Gwatkin does not approve of it. But the triumph of Athanasius over Arius was not primarily due to any of the three causes suggested by Gwatkin's description of Arianism. As a logical system of thought, it is not evidently inferior to

[1] H. M. Gwatkin, *Studies of Arianism* (2nd edn, 1900), p. 274.

that of Athanasius. It has been claimed that Arius' description of Christ as 'a creature but not as one of the creatures' is clear evidence of illogicality.[1] That it is a paradoxical way of speaking is true enough, but it is no more paradoxical than the assertion of Athanasius that, 'as man, Christ knows not, though divinely, being in the Father Word and Wisdom, he knows and there is nothing that he does not know'.[2] In respect of tradition, Arius claimed to be giving expression to the faith of his forefathers in the Church. His claim to be doing so was not markedly inferior to that of his opponents—especially when they chose to rest their case so heavily on the thoroughly untraditional term *homoousios*. In scriptural exegesis also, the difference between the two sides was not so sharply marked as is often assumed. The appeal to the Old Testament is equally unconvincing on both sides.[3] Athanasius' appeal to the New Testament does seem to be more broadly based than that of Arius, but the difference even there is hardly decisive. The really decisive factor was that Athanasius' system clearly presented Christ as a fully divine saviour in a way that Arianism failed to do. If popular piety believed in a Christ who could be worshipped, it believed still more fervently in a Christ who was a divine saviour. It was

[1] T. E. Pollard, 'The Origins of Arianism', *J.T.S.* n.s. IX (1958), 110.
[2] Athanasius, *Or. Con. Ar.* 3.46.   [3] See p. 52 above.

in the effective meeting of this underlying religious need that the secret of Athanasius' victory over Arius lay. The centrality of this point was recognized not only by the popular supporters of Athanasius but by Athanasius himself. He returns to the issue time and again. The point is made in its simplest form by the clear affirmation that created beings cannot be saved by one who is himself a created being.[1] The case is argued more fully and more carefully when it is claimed that such divinity as the Son possesses according to the Arian account of him is his only by participation in that of the Father and not by virtue of his own inherent nature and that therefore it cannot be conveyed to others.[2]

This same fundamental conviction that the touchstone of Christian doctrine was its presentation of Christ as a fully divine saviour was the primary driving force in all Alexandrian theology throughout the fourth and early fifth centuries. It determined Athanasius' attitude not only towards Arius but also towards the Christology of the Antiochene school. If Christ was made up of the divine Word conjoined to a man and not of the Word become flesh, then, Athanasius argued, man is once again robbed of a fully divine saviour. The same insistence is a paramount feature in the teaching of Apollinarius. He could not accept the measure of separation between the human and the divine in

[1] *Ad Adelphium*, 8. [2] *De Synodis*, 51. Cf. *Or. Con. Ar.* 2. 67–70.

the life of Jesus which he encountered in the teaching of the Antiochenes. For if there was anything human about Jesus it was his death; yet it is his death into which we are baptized, it is his death which above all has saving efficacy—and how can the death of a man save us? But Apollinarius presses the point home in still more radical fashion. The rational soul of every human being is by nature changeable (τρεπτός), fallible, unstable, a prisoner of corrupt imaginations, constantly succumbing to the flesh which it ought to be controlling. It is from this condition that man needs to be saved. But if Christ had a human soul or mind, then he would have become enmeshed in this morass of change and fallibility; he could not have been a saviour from it. What man requires for salvation is the replacement of his changeable soul or mind with one that is by nature unchangeable. Only so can the flesh be reduced to its rightful place as the passive instrument in the partnership of soul and body. This, therefore, was what happened in the person of Christ. He did not have a distinct human soul or mind; in him the place of soul or mind was taken instead by a mind that was divine and wholly free from all frustration and change, namely by the Logos himself. Thus and thus only, he argued, could man's salvation be understood, as it must be understood if it is to be salvation at all, as being truly and effectively the work of God.

These basic soteriological arguments had further implications for the Alexandrian mind outside the sphere of the doctrine of the person of Christ. Athanasius could use essentially the same argument which he had used against the Arians with relation to the person of Christ to convince the Tropici that having once affirmed the divinity of Christ they could not stop there but must go on to assert also the divinity of the Spirit. An appeal to the use of the threefold name at baptism was more than an appeal to a magic formula. The Spirit's work of sanctification, in baptism and beyond, involved making men sharers of the divine nature, involved their divinization. If the Spirit was not himself of a fully divine nature, Athanasius argued, he could not conceivably make us partakers of it.[1]

So far the influence of soteriological thinking has been presented as pointing in precisely the same direction as the fact of Christian worship. Its influence was to enhance the divine status ascribed to the person of Christ and to the Holy Spirit. If this tendency had been unchecked by other influences, the Church would undoubtedly have developed a wholly monophysite doctrine and piety in which no place would have been left for Christ in his human nature. The writings of the last years of Augustine's life are a salutary warning of the disastrous results which follow from allowing

[1] *Ep. ad. Ser.* 1.24. For the Tropici, see pp. 31-2 above.

to this soteriological principle an untrammelled power in doctrinal thought. For it is the same principle of the absolutely and exclusively divine nature of saving grace which unchecked gave rise to the enormities of Augustine's final teaching about predestination.

But this influence did not have the field to itself in the Greek church of the fourth century, even in the realm of soteriological ideas. Its impact was strongest in Alexandria, where the allegorical method was the dominant form of scriptural exegesis. In centres like Antioch a greater emphasis on the literal sense of Scripture made it less easy to forget the historical facts of the human life of Jesus. But it is very doubtful if a sense of historical realism alone would have been enough to check the headlong rush of Alexandrian theology in the direction of monophysitism. Indeed, historical realism, in anything like the sense which those words convey today, would be a most misleading description of the ethos of the Antiochene school. Reaction to the excesses of Alexandrian allegorizing was not the major factor in determining Antiochene opposition to the monophysite trend in Alexandrian theology. The basis of the Antiochene approach was as strongly soteriological as the Alexandrian, but it was a different soteriological principle that was dominant in the thought of the Antiochenes. The basic axiom of their thought is best summed up in the famous words of Gregory of Nazianzus that 'what Christ has not assumed he has not healed'.[1] For if it be an essential belief of the genuinely religious mind that the source of salvation must be God himself, it is hardly less essential to be able to believe that that salvation reaches to the point of human need. This second conviction tends clearly to point in a different direction from the first. But before we attempt to describe its central importance for Antiochene theology, we must go back to trace its origins in the preceding centuries.

The greatest challenge to the Church in the second century was the challenge of Gnosticism. Its basic appeal (if we may leave on one side for our present purposes the lunatic fringe of the Gnostic underworld) was that, whatever its eccentricities, it did present Christ unmistakably as a divine saviour. It is a serious mistake to think of the Gnostics as concerned only with cosmological speculation in contrast to the orthodox as people concerned with the saving realities of the religious life. Though the Gnostics were certainly more given to speculation, they were just as concerned with the issues of salvation as was the Church. If, therefore, their beliefs were to be countered effectively, they had to be met at the soteriological level.

In the writings of Irenaeus and Tertullian we find the docetism of the Gnostics, according to

[1] *Epistola*, 101.7.

which Christ's human existence was a matter of appearance rather than of reality, vigorously attacked on the grounds of its inadequate soteriology. The basic affirmation of these early anti-Gnostic writers is that in order to save us Christ must have become what we are, giving his soul for our souls, his flesh for our flesh.[1] It is in the writings of Tertullian that this reasoning is to be found in its most emphatic form. He continually insists that Christ's taking of our flesh was the necessary means of that flesh's purification and ultimate redemption.[2] He does not lay any equivalent stress upon the fact of Christ's taking a human soul, because that was not a bone of contention between him and the majority of the Gnostics. 'The salvation of the soul,' he writes, 'I believe needs no discussion; for almost all heretics, in whatever way they accept it, at least do not deny it. We may leave to his own devices the one solitary Lucan, who spares not even this entity.'[3] But it is clear enough that he regarded Christ's possession of a human soul as the necessary ground for the salvation of our souls.

The fundamental nature of the soteriological principle to which Tertullian appeals is clearly revealed by the fact that it was also held by his Gnostic opponents. Different as their conclusions

[1] Irenaeus, *Adv. Haer.* 5.1.1.   [2] *De Carne Christi*, 16.
[3] *De Res. Carn.* 2.

might be, the principle they shared in common. In Valentinian theory there were three categories of people, those of a spiritual nature (*pneumatikoi*), those of a mid-way animal or soul-like nature (*psuchikoi*) and those of a material or earthy nature (*choïkoi*). The Saviour came to rescue all the *pneumatikoi* and as many of the *psuchikoi* as would respond to him; to that end he himself assumed both a *pneumatikos* and a *psuchikos* nature. The reason he did not assume a *choïkos* nature was precisely that the *choïkoi* were not salvable.[1] Theodotus indeed used the very word *homoousios* to make this point, as orthodoxy was to do some two hundred years later. The body of Jesus which the Christ took was *homoousios* with the Church which he came to save.[2]

This same basic soteriological principle is clearly enunciated by Origen and applied to each part of our human make-up: body, soul and spirit. 'The whole man', said Origen, 'would not have been saved unless Christ had taken upon him the whole man.'[3] But in the years following Origen, the belief that Christ possessed a human soul fell

[1] Irenaeus, *Adv. Haer.* 1.6.1 (describing the system of Ptolemaeus).
[2] Clement, *Excerpta ex Theodotou*, 42.3. *Homoousios* here must mean 'of the same nature as'; it should not be understood as implying an ultra-realistic understanding of the idea of the Church as the body of Christ, as is done by H. E. W. Turner, *The Pattern of Christian Truth*, p. 163. (Compare also *Exc. ex Theod.* 58.2, where ὁμοούσια is most likely to be the right reading.)
Dial. with Herakleides, 136.

into disrepute, though not to the degree of being officially disclaimed. The reasons for this reaction, and for its moderation, have been considered in an earlier chapter.[1] The soteriological grounds on which the belief had first been promulgated were not denied; they were simply left in abeyance. Men were content to speak simply in general terms of the Word becoming man in order to save us men, but the measure of identification was not pressed to apply explicitly to each distinct element in the make-up of the human person. The issue remained effectively in suspense until the time of Apollinarius.

The teaching of Apollinarius represented the first direct and explicit attack upon the idea of Christ's possession of a human soul. Moreover, that attack was, as we have seen, grounded in the soteriological conviction that only a Christ free of the contaminated encumbrance of a human soul could be a truly divine saviour. The decisive factor in the Antiochene reply was the reiteration of the old anti-Gnostic principle as a counterbalancing argument of the same soteriological character. 'He gave his body for men's bodies, his soul for men's souls.'[2] This was not the only argument used against the teaching of Apollinarius but it was, in my judgement, the one of crucial importance.

So successful was this line of argument that it was impossible after that time to attempt to deny

[1] See pp. 56-9 above. [2] Ps.-Athanasius, *Con. Apoll.* 1.17.

that Christ had a human soul. However difficult
it might be for the Alexandrians to fit the idea into
their theological systems, a place had to be found
for it. Cyril readily affirms its existence but allows
it only a passive role in the life of Jesus; in that way
his acceptance of the idea was not allowed to inter-
fere with the underlying scheme of thought which
he had inherited from Athanasius. An important
aspect of the debate between Cyril and Nestorius
was whether such an acceptance of the idea of
Christ's human soul was sufficient to satisfy the
canon of soteriological requirement. For Cyril,
Christ had taken a human soul and that fact by
itself was sufficient to ensure that salvation had
been wrought effectively within the sphere of a full
human nature. But for Nestorius it was important
that the human soul of Jesus should have been
actively engaged in the temptations and emotional
struggles of the incarnate life and have emerged un-
scathed and victorious over them. As the Epistle to
the Hebrews (iv. 14–16) puts it, it is a high priest
who has himself suffered by being tempted who is
able to succour those who are tempted. Soteriology was at the heart of the Nestorian case as
certainly as it was central to Cyril's. If Cyril insisted that it was only the divine Word who could
save and that he must therefore be the subject of
all the actions of the Christ, Nestorius was equally
convinced that it was only a salvation actively

worked out in and through a real human life that could be of practical help to mankind.

From this brief survey it is clear that two great soteriological principles played an immensely important part in the doctrinal debates of the fourth and fifth centuries. On the one hand was the conviction that a saviour must be fully divine; on the other was the conviction that what is not assumed is not healed. Or, to put the matter in other words, the source of salvation must be God; the locus of salvation must be man. It is quite clear that these two principles often pulled in opposite directions. The Council of Chalcedon was the Church's attempt to resolve, or perhaps rather to agree to live with, that tension. Indeed to accept both principles as strongly as did the early Church is already to accept the Chalcedonian faith.

If, then, these two principles are of such paramount importance, we must not shirk a critical examination of them and of their outworking in the early doctrinal debates. How, we must ask, can we be so sure of the truth of these two axioms —that only a fully divine saviour can save and that what is not assumed is not healed? Are they necessary presuppositions for all theological reasoning? Certainly they can be stated in a form which makes them appear to be self-evident propositions. That only God can be the author of ultimate salvation seems to follow necessarily from any adequate understanding of the word 'God'. Similarly it seems to follow from the very meaning of the word 'salvation' that it must reach down to where man is. But when stated in this bare form the axioms are of little value for determining the true expression of Christian doctrine. We may still ask whether it would not be possible for God to be the ultimate author of salvation and man the recipient without the agent or mediator of that salvation being himself necessarily of a fully divine or fully human nature—let alone both.

Any more precise evaluation of this line of patristic argument must take careful account of the prevailing idea of salvation in terms of which it was developed. The dominant concept of salvation in this context was that of being 'made partakers of the divine nature' (2 Pet. i. 4)—in a word, of divinization. 'Because of his immeasurable love he became what we are, that he might fit us to be what he is.'[1] 'He entered into humanity that we might be made divine.'[2] But when they spoke in these terms the Fathers did not intend the parallelism to be taken with full seriousness. The Word, who was fully God, did not become fully man that he might make us full men become fully God. In speaking of man's divinization the Fathers intended to convey that men should become gods only in a secondary sense—'gods by grace' (θεοὶ κατὰ χάριν)

---

[1] Irenaeus, *Adv. Haer.* 5, praef.　　[2] Athanasius, *De Inc.* 54.

was the phrase they used; it was never believed that they would become what the Word was—namely, 'God by nature' (θεὸς κατὰ φύσιν). In the light of this understanding of man's destiny, it does not seem logically absurd to claim on behalf of Arianism that the Son, the supreme God's agent in creation, who in the Arian scheme is the example *par excellence* of what it is to be a 'god by grace' should be able in the work of redemption to bring us to be what he already is and so make us also 'gods by grace' with as full a fellowship with God as is possible for finite beings. It may be that Arius was lacking in soteriological concern and never made such claims; our evidence is far too scanty in substance and too much derived from the polemical writings of opponents for us to have any confidence on that score. But the question is strictly irrelevant to the issue in hand. That issue is whether, even in the light of his own understanding of salvation, the Athanasian argument from the requirements of soteriology is as convincing as he believed it to be and as it has generally been regarded ever since.

In similar vein it may be questioned whether there is any logical absurdity in saying that the Apollinarian Christ in taking human flesh has effected such an important point of contact with men as to enable him to be their saviour. It is generally argued that such a scheme implies a crudely physical conception of salvation and that it would indeed provide salvation only for the flesh. 'It leaves', says Dr Prestige, 'no scope for direct action of the Saviour on the souls of men.'[1] There remains in such a scheme, it is implied, an unbridged gap between the divine saviour and the souls of men who are to be the recipients of that salvation.

But can a gap of some kind in fact be avoided? The majority of those who emphasized the incarnation as the necessary and effective point of man's divinization were men who stressed the corporate nature of Christ's humanity. Irenaeus interpreted the Lucan genealogy, which traces Christ's birth back through seventy-two generations to Adam the son of God, as showing him to be one who summed up in himself all races and all generations of mankind.[2] Cyril of Alexandria with his Platonist background similarly saw the incarnation as an assumption of humanity in general rather than as the becoming of a man. Thereby they could interpret Christ as divinizing mankind as a single entity. But the idea has its difficulties, as clearly as has the closely correlative notion of the fall of all mankind through the sin of the single corporate personality of Adam. Even when Christ's humanity was thought of in such fully corporate terms, a problem remained. The fruit of Adam's

[1] G. L. Prestige, *Fathers and Heretics* (1948), p. 113. [2] *Adv. Haer.* 3. 22. 3.

disobedience was universal in effect. The full fruit of Christ's obedience was not universal. It was taught by some that immortality itself was effectively won for saint and sinner alike by Christ's incarnation, death and resurrection; but an immortal blessedness was not believed to be thus universally or automatically conveyed. Some further link—faith, baptism, eucharistic food—was needed for the fruit of Christ's universal work to become effective in the souls of individual men. It is therefore natural to ask whether the principle that only the divine can save applies also in the same way to this further stage in the effective transmission of salvation. Apollinarius clearly believed that it should. He taught that, since the eucharistic flesh is life-giving, it cannot itself be anything less than divine flesh, the body of the Word imbued with all the divine properties of the Word himself.[1] No gap between the divine and human must be allowed at that point; that which actually conveys salvation to us must itself be fully divine.

These soteriological arguments are at their strongest when salvation is thought of as divinization and when Christ's humanity is understood in corporate terms. Even then there are difficulties in the application of the principle, especially with regard to the effective transmission of that salvation

[1] H. Lietzmann, *Apollinaris und seine Schule*, Frag. 116 (p. 235). Cf. also Gregory of Nyssa, *Or. Cat.* 37.

to the individual souls of men and women. But if we think of salvation as personal knowledge of God and if we think of Christ as having become a man rather than assuming humanity in some abstract, universal sense, then those difficulties are greatly enhanced. For, if salvation be thought of in personal terms, then its effective outworking is through the experience of divine grace in the human soul. Whatever media may be involved, the locus of salvation is the sphere of ordinary personal existence in which God establishes fellowship with man. Is this experience of divine grace, then, a meeting of the fully divine and the fully human of the kind which the soteriological principle defines as a necessary precondition for the realization of man's salvation? Difficulties arise whatever answer we give to that question. In one sense the experience of divine grace is a meeting of the human and the divine. But if we return an affirmative answer to our question, the whole argument of the Fathers falls to the ground. For it was of the essence of Athanasius' case against the early Antiochenes that on soteriological grounds Christ must be unique and not just the supreme example of saint or prophet; the heart of the soteriological argument was that it required there to be in Christ a meeting of the fully divine and the fully human which is different in kind from that which characterizes the experience of divine grace in ordinary human life.

But if we therefore return a negative answer, a different problem arises. Why should the axioms of salvation which we have been considering be a requisite condition in the primary archetypal instance of the life of Christ but not be applicable to the outworking in contemporary human experience of the salvation which he brought? If salvation be understood to be that personal knowledge of God which is open to man through divine grace, can its achievement require as of logical necessity the prior existence of a divine-human meeting of a radically different and superior kind?

I do not wish to suggest that the soteriological arguments of the Fathers are totally invalid. We ought always to hesitate before declaring that convictions which have been so strongly held are sheer unadulterated mistake. Such cases are more commonly a matter of true insights wrongly applied. Like the classical arguments for the existence of God, our axioms may be quite invalid when regarded as a form of deductive reasoning and yet still retain insights of importance. It may be impossible to argue that for Christ to be saviour he must have been of such and such a nature. Yet there may still be a logical connexion of a looser kind between the nature of Christ and the salvation that he brought—the kind of connexion which might be described as a relation of suitability or fittingness. This would imply that there is most certainly a significant connexion between the nature of Christ's person and his work of salvation. If salvation be conceived in personal terms, such a connexion indeed can hardly be doubted. But it would be a connexion of such a kind that the soteriological significance of Christ's personal nature would be something which could only be recognized when that nature had first become clear to us through other means; it would not be something which could be used directly to determine what the nature of Christ's person must have been. In that case it would no longer be open to us to give to the soteriological arguments of the Fathers the same kind of value which the Fathers themselves ascribed to them.

6

THE FORM OF THE
ARGUMENTS

THE doctrinal writings of the Fathers of the
second half of the fourth century appear to
us to be of a highly intellectual and speculative character. So indeed they are. But the evidence which we have considered so far has shown
clearly enough that they were much more than an
intellectual pastime, much more than the enjoyable
exercise of the speculative imagination. In the eyes
of the Fathers the presence of heresy made the task
of doctrinal definition inevitable, while the close
relation which they believed to exist between the
doctrines being defined and the way of salvation
made it not only an inevitable task but a vitally
important one as well.

In the last three chapters we have been concerned with the main sources of doctrinal reasoning.[1] But there is more to an argument than its

---

[1] It may seem surprising that I have not included 'tradition' among
these main sources of doctrinal reasoning. The ideas normally brought
together under this heading are in fact touched upon at various points.
In the second century 'tradition' is not a distinct entity in separation
from Scripture (see chapter 3). The most significant extra-canonical
traditions were those of the *lex orandi* (see chapter 4). The idea of
loyalty to tradition as loyalty to the formulated teaching of earlier
generations is considered in chapter 7.

source. We need to consider not only the grounds to which appeal was made, but also the way in which such appeals were conducted; not only the basis of the argument but also the pattern of argumentation is important.

The framework of thought in terms of which early doctrine was developed was provided by Greek philosophy. Our own approach to Christian faith is so firmly rooted in that tradition that it is not easy for us to imagine how it could ever have been otherwise. Père Daniélou's book *Théologie du Judéo-Christianisme*, recently translated into English as *The Theology of Jewish Christianity*, is a useful aid towards such an act of historical imagination. It gives us a glimpse into a different world, a world in which the framework of thought is the imagery of Jewish apocalyptic. It is a strange world. As a setting for theological ideas, it is vigorous, pictorial and imaginative, but wildly unsystematic and to our ears, at least, often strangely bizarre. It may be that it was primarily historical reasons that determined that the world of Hellenistic ideas rather than that of Jewish apocalyptic should be the cradle of early Christian doctrine. If so, it is a historical fact about which we need have no regrets.

But if we turn back from such a glimpse of a Jewish apocalyptic interpretation of Christianity with a renewed sense of gratitude for the Church's heritage of Greek thought, it must not make us blind to the dangers and shortcomings of the latter. The debate about the so-called Hellenization of Christian thought has too often been conducted in absolutist terms, as if we must choose between regarding Hellenism either as the perfect vehicle for Christian thought, providing a 'language fitted, as none other ever has been, to furnish an exact and permanent terminology for doctrinal purposes' or else as a *damnosa hereditas* holding 'the key of the prison-house of many souls'.[1] We do not have to choose between saying either, on the one hand, that Christianity has been the undisputed master, using the traditions of classical philosophy perfectly and exclusively for its own purposes, as Moses reputedly did with the wisdom of the Egyptians, or on the other that, like the lean kine of Pharaoh's dream, philosophy has swallowed whole the healthier growth of Christian faith. No pattern of human thought is ideally suited to express the full riches of Christian truth and Christian experience. Every idiom has its own particular disadvantages, and we must not shrink from trying to recognize and assess them.

I do not intend to undertake a detailed examination of the impact of particular philosophical ideas

[1] The phrases are taken from C. Gore, *The Incarnation of the Son of God* (1891), p. 105, and E. Hatch, *The Influence of Greek Ideas and Usages upon the Christian Church* (1890), p. 138, respectively.

upon the formulation of Christian doctrine. That is a subject of great importance and of great complexity. But it is also possible to approach the question in a much more general way. The primary influence of Greek ideas on the thinking of the Church was of a non-technical kind. The main trend of contemporary philosophical thought was eclectic in character. Differences between the varying schools were still of importance, but they were of secondary importance. It is the underlying approach, which was common to the differing schools, that is of primary significance. If Platonism was a dominant element in this tradition, it was Platonism of a markedly developed and diluted kind. Its fundamental characteristic was its ontology, its approach to and understanding of what is truly real. The function of philosophic reflexion was to distinguish between the visible phenomena of the physical world and the eternal essences which lie behind them. It was to these essences, approached not by the senses but by a process of intellection, that the highest reality and the highest value were to be ascribed. The significance of such a scheme of thought as the framework of theological thinking is obvious. It suggests an approach to theology in which its affirmations are regarded as descriptive accounts (albeit very imperfect accounts) of ultimate realities existing in the spiritual world. The fact that patristic theology grew up against such a background gave to it an ontological urge and an ontological confidence which are both its glory and its weakness.

My aim in this chapter is to point to some of the consequences which followed from this general approach to theology. But it must be emphasized at the outset that most of the tendencies to which I shall point are not ones which could only have arisen under the influence of Greek ideas. The tendency to objectify is not the exclusive prerogative of the Greek metaphysician. The basic issues with which I shall be concerned are dangers which are inherent in any form of systematic thought. Nevertheless, it is still true that the metaphysical temper of Greek philosophy, which did in fact colour the approach of so many of the Fathers, was such as to make them peculiarly vulnerable to the dangers inherent in such a systematization of theological ideas.

We may begin with a simple example. At the last supper Jesus spoke of the bread which he gave to his disciples as his body. Paul in his epistles wrote of the Church as the body of Christ. Both concepts are rich in religious meaning and have entered deeply into the piety of Christians throughout the ages. In neither instance is it self-evident that the statement is a definition, whose meaning can be properly elucidated in terms of substance and of accidents. Yet that in course of time is how the former affirmation has come to be regarded. Even though the particular doctrine of transubstantiation with which the Western church is most familiar belongs to a later period, yet its essential spirit was fully developed within the patristic age. Christian writers of the second and third centuries use with equal freedom the directly realistic language of Jesus himself and the language of symbolism. They lived in a world in which the idea of symbol is a thoroughly positive concept, embodying rather than standing over against that which it symbolizes. The same spirit lived on in the fourth century but with it went also the beginnings of an attempt at definition of a very different kind. Gregory of Nyssa argues that as in the body of the incarnate Christ bread was transformed into body by the process of digestion, so now the bread used at the eucharist is transformed (or, more precisely, to use Gregory's word, 'transelemented') into the body of Christ instantaneously at the prayer of consecration.[1] The issue which divided Monophysite and Dyophysite, those who insisted respectively on the unity and duality of natures in Christ, when it came to a question of their understanding of the eucharist was whether or not after the moment of consecration the bread continued to

[1] *Or. Cat.* 37 (μεταποιεῖσθαι and μεταστοιχειοῦσθαι are the terms used).

possess its former substance, appearance and form.[1] There is no need here to consider the subtle variations of expression used by different writers in their development of such ideas once the issues had been raised in this way. The prior question is whether the whole form of discussion is appropriate to the subject-matter in hand.

It might seem that for those who would return a negative answer to that question the nature of the task awaiting them would be quite simple. Its detailed outworking would no doubt prove difficult enough, but its general form would be clear—a replacement of the ontological approach in those spheres of doctrinal development where it has been inappropriately applied. But the task is more complex than that description might suggest. If it be true at all that the natural tendency to objectify has been on occasion misapplied in the outworking of Christian doctrine, the effects of such mis-application cannot be isolated and restricted to a few specific doctrines. Doctrinal development was a long historical process of closely interrelated concepts. The use of wrong method at one point must be expected to have had wide-ranging effect. One of the ways in which this can be seen is the way in which an objectifying temper of mind seeks necessarily to bring co-ordinate aspects of religious

[1] Theodoret, *Eranistes Dial.* II (*P.G.* 83, 168c). (οὐσία, σχῆμα and εἶδος are the words used.)

truth into formal relationship with one another. In the realm of symbolic thought, a considerable profusion of imagery can co-exist fruitfully. There is a danger that the more philosophically minded systematizer may combine such varied imagery in a way that is positively misleading. An illustration can be given from the same realm of eucharistic theology.

In the rich and variegated thought of the earliest Christian writers about the eucharist, two themes stand out as of primary importance. These are the ideas of spiritual food and of sacrifice. Both ideas figure, for example, in the teaching of Justin, who is our fullest early witness upon the subject. In development of the first idea Justin can speak quite directly of the bread and wine of the eucharist as the body and blood of Christ which we receive for the nourishment of our spiritual lives.[1] With regard to the idea of sacrifice, Justin (like so many of the early Christian writers) quotes the prophecy of Mal. i. 11, 'From the rising of the sun even unto the going down of the same my name is great among the Gentiles; and in every place incense is offered unto my name, and a pure offering', and claims that its fulfilment is to be seen in the Christian eucharist. Its character as a pure offering or sacrifice is seen in two ways. On the one hand Justin agrees with his Jewish opponent Trypho (and with many other of the most religious spirits of the

[1] *Apol.* i.61.

age, whether Gentile or Jewish) 'that prayers and thanksgivings, when offered by worthy men, are the only perfect and well-pleasing sacrifices to God'.[1] On the other hand, the bread and the wine themselves can also be seen as the pure offering; they are, in Irenaeus' words, the first-fruits of God's creation offered back to him as a token of man's gratitude.[2]

Each of these concepts has a clear and distinctive meaning of its own. They bring out different aspects of what is happening in the religious reality of eucharistic worship. But if each be treated as an ontological affirmation describing in some absolute sense the nature of the eucharistic elements and of the eucharistic action, then it becomes natural to co-ordinate them in a new way. If the elements *are* the body and blood of Christ and the offering *is* a sacrifice, then the eucharist as a whole must be a sacrificial offering of the body and blood of Christ. This concept we find explicitly affirmed in the teaching of Cyprian. But the composite idea thus created is in fact something very different from the ideas of the two component parts before they had been thus combined.[3]

It is my contention that this kind of combination of concepts without reference to their contextual difference is a very dangerous form of theological

[1] *Dial.* 117.   [2] *Ibid.* 41.3; Irenaeus, *Adv. Haer.* 4.18.4.
[3] See my 'Theological Legacy of St Cyprian', *J.E.H.* XIV (1963), 147–8.

construction. No doubt there were various causes which helped to give rise to the particular development in eucharistic theology which I have described. But undoubtedly one factor in the situation was the oversimplified way in which theological statements were thought of as being descriptive of corresponding spiritual realities. Whatever other motives may have been at work, this mode of understanding theology contributed significantly to the form of theological expression and the manner of subsequent interpretation.

This approach to theological ideas has its effect also on the way in which thought about a particular doctrine is liable to develop over a considerable period of time. If one believes that the result of successful doctrinal discussion is the attainment of an objective knowledge of clearly definable religious entities, then that knowledge will be thought of as a secure and permanent possession for all time. It will be regarded as the assured result of theological endeavour and as valid in all situations and in all contexts. It will be natural to assert the truth of such doctrinal conclusions absolutely without reference to the arguments by which they were established and to look upon them as a secure foundation upon which further work of theological construction can be built. Such procedure appears at first sight a natural enough method of advance for the development of a well-grounded theological system. But it is open to serious criticism. For if it be permissible to accept the results of the first stage of a theological inquiry as established without need for further reference to the means by which those results were secured, there is a danger that the arguments used in the second stage of the inquiry may be logically incompatible with those used in the first, and that that inconsistency may remain wholly undetected. Something of this kind does seem to have happened in the fundamental question of trinitarian doctrine.

The primary emphasis of the theologians of the second and third centuries was the demonstration of the distinct existence of the three persons of the godhead. The chief enemy was the popular Monarchianism of a modalist kind which blurred or denied the reality of those distinctions. Origen might claim that belief in the existence of the three distinct persons belonged to the apostolic deposit of faith, but in face of the presence of modalist thinking in the Church the issue was one which called for clear proof. Such proof needed to do more than point to the difference of name, since no one was denying that obvious fact; it needed to establish what kind of difference was indicated by the difference of name.

One of the pieces of evidence to which the anti-modalist writers most frequently point is the way in which Scripture speaks of God as invisible but

THE FORM OF THE ARGUMENTS

also as being seen by men. Either, therefore, the
Scriptures are guilty of self-contradiction or else
there must be two distinct beings to whom the
name God·is rightly given—the one visible, the
other invisible.[1] In similar vein Tertullian goes on
to produce a whole list of Johannine texts which
speak of the Son as sent by the Father, receiving
authority from him and praying to him.[2] The
heart of his attack upon Praxeas is summed up in
the jibe that his theology involved the blasphemous
concept that the Father was crucified.[3] This was the
shaft that went home more surely than any other.
Ever afterwards Modalist Monarchianism was
known in the West as Patripassianism, the heresy
that taught the suffering of the Father.

So the modalist heresy was discredited and
defeated. The distinct nature of the three divine
persons could be regarded as firmly established.
By the middle of the fourth century the issue at
stake had changed. The main efforts of the Catholic
theologians at that later stage were directed against
a very different foe. The Arian tradition did not
deny the reality of the three divine persons. Its
error, in orthodox eyes, was that it denied their
co-equality and regarded them as a descending
hierarchy of beings. Against such a foe the
arguments which had served Tertullian so well

[1] Tertullian, *Adv. Prax.* 14; Novatian, *De Trinitate*, 18.
[2] *Adv. Prax.* 21–5.   [3] *Ibid.* 1.

against Praxeas were a positive embarrassment. If the distinction between the Father and the Son lies in the fact that the one is invisible and the other visible, they can hardly be co-equal persons in the one godhead. (Even Tertullian had been conscious of a weakness in his own argument at this point, and having once made it contradicts himself in the same chapter of the *Adversus Praxeam* by asserting that the Son, as Spirit and Word of God, is invisible and that the Old Testament records of men who saw God ought to be understood to refer to dreams and visions.[1]) Moreover, the same Johannine texts about the sending and authorizing of the Son by the Father which Tertullian had used to indicate his distinctiveness from the Father were used by the Arians as evidence of his inferiority.[2] Later writers therefore found themselves forced to deny the applicability of such texts to the relation of the Father and the Son altogether. Engaged as they were on the second stage of the theological enterprise, it seemed to them that if such words were allowed to refer to the Father and the Son as divine beings, they would play straight into the hands of the Arians; they would furnish dangerous evidence in support of the Son's inferiority to the Father. Ignoring the fact, therefore, that such an interpretation of those texts was a part of the ground upon which they themselves were

[1] *Adv. Prax.* 14.   [2] See Athanasius, *Or. Con. Ar.* 3. 7, 26.

standing, they insisted that they did not refer to the relation of the first two persons of the Trinity at all but to the relation of the Father and the incarnate Christ.

It is clear that the development of the doctrine has passed through two distinct stages. In the first stage differences between the persons of the Trinity are recognized and on the strength of these differences the distinctness of the persons is established. In the second stage the full co-equality of the three persons is established by denying all differences between them, necessarily including those differences which were the initial evidence for asserting the distinct existence of the three persons. This process therefore involves not merely the forgetting but the practical repudiation of the lines of argument used at the earlier stage. If we put together the basic reasoning of the ante-Nicene and the post-Nicene periods, the outcome reads something like this: To fail to distinguish the persons of the Father and the Son and thereby to involve the Father in the experiences of the incarnation is to commit the enormity of Patripassianism, involving the impassible Father in suffering. The incarnation and the crucifixion must therefore be affirmed of the Son—who is co-equally impassible with the Father.

It may be claimed in reply that all that has been said so far can readily be admitted without in any way invalidating the eventual outcome of the whole process. The struggle with Arianism, it may be argued, showed up a weakness in much of Tertullian's reasoning. It is not uncommon for a pioneer in thought (particularly one of Tertullian's temperament) to overstate his case. When the faulty elements have been removed, there would still be a sufficient remainder to establish the anti-modalist case. But the answer is less cogent than at first sight it appears. For in the final development of the doctrine of the fully co-equal Trinity at the hands of the Cappadocian Fathers (Basil of Caesarea, Gregory of Nazianzus and Gregory of Nyssa), it is insisted that there can be no point of difference or variation whatever in the operation of the three persons; it is the perfect identity of their operations which is the guarantee of their unity of being. If the principle that the persons of the Trinity never act towards the world in separation from one another (*opera trinitatis ad extra sunt indivisa*) be accepted as a summary of orthodox conviction on the matter, then only one kind of argument is left open for the establishment of the anti-modalist case by which the distinctness of the persons is demonstrated. It cannot be derived from reflexion upon or response to the divine activity at all; it can only be known if it has been imparted to us as a verbal disclosure about the inner nature of the godhead in Scripture or the apostolic tradition. On one occasion after recalling, as he does so frequently, the baptismal formula, Basil declares simply that 'the names signify things'.[1] It was not intended to be a comprehensive statement of Cappadocian epistemology. Yet it does give succinct expression to what in fact has, for them, to be the case. It is the names—not the activities, for in that respect they are not to be distinguished—it is the names alone which tell us of the differences of person. It is much more than the aberrations of Tertullian's excessive zeal against the Modalists that has to be abandoned. Patristic reasoning about the Trinity can only be saved from the charge of inconsistency by allowing that it is grounded on an appeal to Scripture of a kind which is totally at variance with one that would find general acceptance in the modern world.[2]

This discussion of trinitarian doctrine arose out of an attempt to understand the logical structure of the development of a doctrine through two distinct stages; it was designed to show that the reasoning used in those stages, though apparently convincing when each stage is regarded in isolation, may prove to be self-contradictory when the two are put together and seen as part of a single process of development. But trinitarian doctrine has a

[1] Basil, *Ep.* 210.4.
[2] See my 'Some Reflections on the Origins of the Doctrine of the Trinity', *J.T.S.* n.s. VIII (1957), 92–106, where the case outlined here is developed in greater detail.

further claim upon our attention as the most notable example of the influence of philosophical ideas on early Christian doctrine. In the case of eucharistic theology it may reasonably be claimed that the language of substance and accidents has simply been misapplied; but the same claim would have less obvious plausibility if made in respect of the doctrine of the Trinity. For if *ousia* be intended to convey the concept of 'being' in its most fundamental sense, then it is not unreasonable for that idea to be brought into relation to the Christian God, who is regarded as the ultimate source of all true being. If we are to assess the positive value and the possible shortcomings of this doctrinal tradition as a whole, it is in the doctrine of God that the most crucial test is to be found. What was the intention of Athanasius and of the Cappadocians when they set out to speak of God in terms of *ousia* and *hupostasis* and how far did they achieve their intention?

I have already argued that the introduction of *ousia* language into Christian thought about the godhead was something forced upon the Church by Arius.[1] Its use by the orthodox at Nicaea had no clear or precise meaning. It was primarily negative in intention. Positively, it was intended to imply that the Son was God in the same full sense that the Father was God. It contributed nothing

[1] See pp. 33–6 above.

towards an understanding of the nature of that unity.[1] Athanasius does not use the term with great frequency in his own writings. It was the experience of the Arian revival of the 350s that led him to insist so firmly on its inescapable necessity. When he argued that not to use it is to depart from scriptural precedent and to imply the non-existence of God, even he cannot have taken his arguments very seriously.[2] His real reasons were practical. Time had shown that nothing else was as decisively exclusive of Arianism. The word *hupostasis*, on the other hand, was a matter of complete indifference to him. He himself regarded it as synonymous with *ousia*,[3] but he was quite prepared to recognize that it was used in differing ways which made it applicable to the one or to the three in the Christian understanding of the godhead.[4] Athanasius was not attempting to give a philosophical account of the godhead and we go astray if we try to interpret his thought in such terms.

But with the Cappadocians it is different. The difference is partly an outcome of their different temperament, partly an outcome of the new situation with which they were faced. For by their day Eunomius had developed the logic of Arius' position in a far more rigorous and thorough-going

---

[1] See G. C. Stead, 'The Significance of the ὁμοούσιος' (Texte und Untersuchungen, 78), *Studia Patristica*, vol. III, part I (1961), pp. 397–412, and my 'ὁμοούσιος ἡμῖν', *J.T.S.* n.s. XVI (1965), 454–61.
[2] *Ad Afros*, 4.   [3] *Ibid.*   [4] *Tomus ad Antiochenos*, 5, 6.

way than Arius himself had ever done. They do, therefore, undertake a determined attempt to give a coherent account of the Christian godhead. They see the one *ousia* and the three *hupostaseis* as concepts necessary to a clear statement of the Christian faith. They do not believe that man can aspire to a full understanding of the godhead (it is indeed one of their basic complaints against Eunomius that he implies that man is able to do so), but they do believe that the idea of the three-in-one can be made sufficiently intelligible to be a vital criterion of true belief. In pursuit of this task they use many analogies and examples in order to clarify the meaning of the vital terms *ousia* and *hupostasis*. Nevertheless, the precise sense in which they themselves understood the words is not at all easy to grasp; it has proved one of the major issues of dispute between historians of doctrine throughout the last century. These differences of interpretation arise from two main sources: a certain ambiguity in the thinking of the Cappadocians themselves and a frequent failure on the part of interpreters to appreciate the radical Platonism which lies at the back of all their thought.

Basil regularly explains the relation of *ousia* to *hupostasis* as that of the common to the particular.[1] He gives many examples of things that share a common *ousia*. He even cites the potter and the

[1] E.g. *Epp.* 214. 4; 236. 6.

clay, and the shipbuilder and the timber, as being *homoousioi* by virtue of their common materiality.[1] But the most significant example is that of human beings, which is still more frequently used by Gregory of Nyssa.[2] All this has given ground to the theory that at heart the Cappadocians were tritheists and that *homoousios* meant for them the sharing of a common divine nature. But this is to interpret their examples in the light of our presuppositions. For them as thoroughgoing Platonists the *ousia* that is common to all men is not an abstract concept but the most real thing that there is. It is this fact, so foreign to our way of thought, that is determinative of their understanding of the divine *ousia* and which shows them to be essentially monotheistic in intention.

Their use of *ousia*, therefore, must be understood from within the setting of a radical Platonism. The problem then arises of the sense to be given to *hupostasis* within the same context. The word did not have the same measure of philosophical tradition behind it. Within a fully Platonist framework any individual concretion of *ousia* must necessarily have a lesser degree of reality than the *ousia* itself. But the Cappadocian intention is certainly to ascribe the same measure of reality to the divine

[1] *Adv. Eun.* 2.19 (*P.G.* 29, 613c).
[2] Basil, *Adv. Eun.* 4 (*P.G.* 29, 681 a b); Basil (really Gregory of Nyssa), *Ep.* 38. 2; Gregory of Nyssa, *On Not Three Gods*.

hupostasis as to the divine *ousia*. Common sense
then as now (without needing to call in any special
Aristotelian influence) tended to regard the particular as just as real as the common—if not more
so. The reaction that to use the analogy of three
men is to imply tritheism is not restricted to the
modern interpreter. It was felt by ordinary people
in their own day and Gregory of Nazianzus has
to deal with the objection in his preaching.[1] The
Cappadocians were therefore far less likely to be
challenged on the score of not giving sufficient
reality to the divine *hupostaseis*. The word *hupostasis* had a long and well-established history as
the term for use in referring to the distinct persons
of the godhead which went right back to Origen.[2]
This fact, together with the common-sense meaning
of the word, naturally gave the impression of
reference to a firm, solid, individual entity. Any
shift of meaning that the term might need to under-
go by virtue of its role in the Cappadocian scheme
of thought as a whole would not be immediately
apparent. It would seem, therefore, that they were
able to assert the full reality of the one divine *ousia*
on technical philosophical grounds and at the same
time to convey a sense of the equal reality of the
three divine *hupostaseis* on common-sense grounds

[1] *Or.* 31, 13.
[2] It is, for example, the Greek word which is translated 'existences'
in the quotation from Origen on p. 22 above.

134

even though these were not strictly compatible with the philosophy to which appeal was being made in the case of the divine *ousia*.

But the difficulties with which the Cappadocians were faced may be put in another way. As Platonists they shared with their opponents the conviction that the divine *ousia* was simple (ἁπλοῦς) and uncompounded (ἀσύνθετος). They insisted, as we saw earlier, on the unity of divine activity as evidence against any division of the divine *ousia*. But the evidence of revelation forced them to modify the strictness with which they applied their principle of the divine simplicity. If it were applied without qualification there was no escape from Arianism. And so they were led to insist that there were distinguishing characteristics in which the three *hupostaseis* differed from one another, but that these did nothing to disrupt the simplicity of the divine *ousia*.[1] The distinguishing marks did not affect the divine activity in the world; they concerned only the relations of the *hupostaseis* to one another. These were differently defined—by Gregory of Nazianzus as ingeneracy, generation and procession; by Gregory of Nyssa as cause, being directly caused, and being indirectly caused. This raises, as we have argued earlier, very serious epistemological difficulties about how such dis-

---

[1] Basil, *Adv. Eun.* 2. 29 (*P.G.* 29,640); Gregory of Nyssa, *Con. Eun.* (ed. Jaeger), 1. 270–81.

tinctions can be known to men. But it raises two further difficulties as well concerning the nature of the distinctions postulated and the claim that they leave the simplicity of the divine essence unaffected.

Gregory of Nyssa unashamedly uses the language of causation to describe the distinctions of the three persons. The same idea is implicit in the more customary terminology of generation and procession. At times the Cappadocians seem to imply that the Father is the source of divinity within the godhead; but this is in flagrant contradiction to the main drift of their position. More probably they should be understood to mean that the Father is the source of the hypostatic existence of the other two, that is, their existence as distinguishable *hupostaseis* or persons. But, even in this more reduced sense, the idea is very difficult to square with the idea of a fully co-equal Trinity which it was their aim to define. A. H. Armstrong commends them for breaking free from 'the basic (and quite arbitrary) assumption of late Greek hierarchic thinking that the product is always inferior to the producer'.[1] But if that is an arbitrary assumption, then it would seem that the very possibility of analogical reasoning is being undermined. It may be that the Cappadocians could say nothing else. To describe the relationship of the

[1] A. H. Armstrong and R. A. Markus, *Christian Faith and Greek Philosophy* (1960), p. 22.

persons in significantly different terms would have been to cease to be interpreters of traditional Christian teaching of a Father-Son relationship within the godhead. But the paradoxical nature of affirming a co-equal Trinity whose members stand to one another in the relation of cause to effect must not be obscured by claiming that the oddity we feel about it is no more than an arbitrary assumption of Greek thought.

But quite apart from the particular nature of the distinctions affirmed, there seems to be an arbitrariness about the claim that they leave the divine simplicity unimpaired. If the unity and simplicity of the divine *ousia* are compatible with its existence in three distinguishable *hupostaseis*, it is difficult to see why they should not be equally compatible with a modalist—or to use the word most commonly used in the Eastern Church, a Sabellian—interpretation also, according to which the one God expresses himself in different modes, now as Father, now as Son, now as Holy Spirit, as his purposes of self-revelation to the world may require. The Cappadocians could argue that since the three *hupostaseis* are eternal and permanent existents, their understanding preserves, as the Sabellian does not, the eternal changelessness of God. It is not easy to feel that they also preserved his full simplicity. In practice thay did not have to concern themselves too much about whether they were weakening the ramparts of defence against Sabellianism. A Sabellian approach to the nature of God, never popular in the Eastern Church, had been finally quashed in the person of Marcellus a generation before. The outstanding opponent of Marcellus at that time had been Eusebius of Caesarea. Eusebius' thought was grounded in the tradition of Origen with its three distinct persons of the godhead in descending hierarchical sequence; despite his reluctant acceptance of the creed of Nicaea, the pattern of Eusebius' thought was not radically different in the years after Nicaea from what it had been in the period before. The quashing of Marcellus, therefore, had been effected from a standpoint which the Cappadocians had totally abandoned. But the fact could conveniently be forgotten. Sabellianism was no longer a living threat. Their real battle was on the other flank. If their ideas did weaken the flank on the opposing wing, there were no Sabellians waiting there to take advantage of the weakness.

What then are we to say of this attempt to give philosophic expression to the Christian idea of God? It is not a case of philosophy winning out over revelation. It is the Cappadocians' attempt to be faithful to the evidence of revelation that leads to the inconsistencies in their thought. Their radical Arian opponent, Eunomius, is not to be seen as the Aristotelian dialectician in contrast to their Platonism; he is to be seen rather as the more determinedly consistent exponent of those same Platonist presuppositions which they also held. It cannot fairly be claimed that they found any philosophical solution to their problem. They simply expressed that problem with the use of philosophical terms. Perhaps that is all a philosophical statement ever does. But the point of doing so is to throw some new light upon the problem in hand. And this they failed to achieve. The most carefully articulated statement of the relation of *ousia* and *hupostasis* remains in the final analysis no less paradoxical than Gregory of Nazianzus' more direct declaration that the Trinity is 'separately one and unitedly separate'.[1]

'That God is one and that the Son is God are truths of revelation which the category of "substance" failed to synthesise,' says Robertson, and quotes with approval Newman's words that the orthodox doctrine is 'not only a contradiction in the terms used, but in our ideas'.[2] Newman goes on to assert that it is 'not therefore a contradiction in fact'. But the real question is what has been gained by restating the problem in the contradictory terms and ideas of *ousia* and *hupostasis*. It was right and necessary in the historical situation

[1] *Or.* 23. 8.
[2] A. Robertson, *Athanasius* (Nicene and Post-Nicene Fathers, 1892), Introduction, pp. xxxii–xxxiii and p. 366, n. 1.

that the attempt should be made. But it may be equally right and necessary to conclude that the outcome of the attempt was to wrap up the nature of the problem in a way which is more likely to mislead than to illuminate. If in attempting to give philosophical expression to conflicting aspects of our experience, we are led to an apparently irreconcilable antinomy in our thinking, we do best to go back to the apparent conflict in experience in the hope that in due course some other form of philosophical expression may throw new light upon our problem. Gregory of Nyssa enunciates the empirical principle that in the physical world experience is superior to theories of causation and argues that similarly in the spiritual realm faith is superior to argumentation. Faith he delineates as 'the faith which teaches us at once the distinction in *hupostasis* and the conjunction in *ousia*'.[1] But the kind of faith which his argument requires is surely one which would speak a less sophisticated language.

[1] Basil (really Gregory of Nyssa), *Ep.* 38.5.

7

THE ASSIMILATION OF
NEW IDEAS

T HE last chapter was an attempt to survey
some aspects of the reasoning of the Fathers
in doctrinal debate. But the aspect of their
thinking which is most directly linked to the
question of the development of doctrine is the way
in which new ideas arose and were related to existing beliefs. Disputants about the theory of development have debated in what sense, if any, it is
proper to speak of the emergence of new ideas at
all. With this broader issue we need not now concern
ourselves. It is self-evident that there was in some
sense an emergence of new insights, whether in the
ultimate analysis they are to be regarded as new
revelation or new understanding of the old. The
question which I wish now to investigate is the
historical question how such new insights were
assimilated and related to old ideas and formulations of belief.

There are two main ways in which new beliefs
can be incorporated into an existing body of ideas.
The most natural initial assumption is that all that
is required is simply to add in the new beliefs

without any modification or alteration of those already held. If this can be satisfactorily done, no problem arises. But very often the new belief does not conveniently fit into the existing pattern of ideas. In that case the new beliefs cannot simply be added in; they have rather to be added on as a series of awkwardly attached appendices. In course of time this results in the development of a very unwieldy system of beliefs. What appears at first sight, therefore, to be the simplest method of taking in the new ideas proves to be far from simple. At this point the second method of dealing with new ideas may prove preferable. If the new beliefs are allowed to modify the existing system of belief, it may then be possible for them to be included without difficulty in a newly revised pattern of thought. At the actual moment of change, this modification of the existing pattern may seem a very revolutionary and even destructive process. But in course of time it will normally come to be seen from a broader perspective as representing a more satisfying, because more far-reaching, syn-thesis. A familiar example of this kind of change is the movement from a Ptolemaic to a Copernican view of the universe. It would have been theoreti-cally possible to continue with the Ptolemaic scheme of interpretation and simply to add on to it an increasingly complex series of qualifying clauses. But the so-called 'Copernican revolution', however apparently destructive of old ideas in its initial impact, was in the long run a far simpler and more satisfactory way of incorporating the new knowledge into the old corpus of beliefs.[1]

The former of these two methods may be called the assimilation of new ideas by the addition of new refinements to the old; the latter may be called the assimilation of new ideas by modification of the old. The bias of the Fathers is undoubtedly towards the former method. To add to what had been said by the heroes of the past need imply no sort of criticism of them; the occasion for the new affirmation might not yet have arisen in their time. But to correct even the form of what they had actually said was felt to imply an unacceptable breach with the tradition in which the Church stood. If, as I have suggested, the Fathers sometimes did contradict the argument of their avowedly orthodox predecessors, it was an unconscious contradiction; it was because they had forgotten the earlier argument and remembered only the conclusions. At the conscious level they were unwilling to admit the need for any change in past formulations; addition might be necessary, but change was not to be admitted. Convinced as he was of the necessity for distinguishing *ousia* and *hupostasis* in the defence of orthodoxy, Basil might

[1] The analogy between doctrinal development and the 'Copernican revolution' is examined more fully in chapter 8. See pp. 169–74 below.

have admitted that the distinction had not been so clearly drawn in the past; he could not bring himself to accept the fact that the creed of Nicaea with its anathema against those 'who assert that the Son of God is of a different *hupostasis* or *ousia*' had actually identified the two terms.[1] Thus the general aim of the Fathers was always to accommodate any new ideas in the way which involved the least possible alteration to the officially formulated notions of the past. In practice the two methods were not always as clearly distinct as I have described them. The facts usually constitute something of a compromise between the two. There was usually some modification of the old pattern but not enough to incorporate the new ideas altogether satisfactorily into a new synthesis. But the degree of modification varies. The far-reaching effect of a difference of method at this point can be illustrated by the comparison of two closely related doctrines whose development is distinctively different on this score.

We have been concerned at a number of points in this inquiry with that basic issue of early doctrinal development—the growth of belief in the full divinity of the Son and in the co-equal Trinity. The emergence of the full trinitarian doctrine was not possible without significant modification of previously accepted ideas. Chris-

[1] *Ep.* 125. 1.

tians began with a clear and well-grounded belief that the Father of Christ was God and that there was and could be only one God. This belief was rooted in the unqualified monotheism of the Old Testament and reinforced, as we have seen, by the Apologists' acceptance of the philosophical idea of an undifferentiated divine unity of an essentially mathematical kind. The Modalist Monarchians might deny the new evidence of the Son's separate existence and the Dynamic Monarchians the new evidence of his divinity. But apart from such denials it was not easy to see how the new evidence could be assimilated at all into the old framework. The contribution of Tertullian and of Origen was not that they provided an immediate solution to that problem but that, very tentatively at least, they pointed in the direction which the Church was to take through the apparent impasse with which she was faced. The line of development which they indicated was in effect the modification of the concept of unity from a primarily mathematical concept to a more organic one. This change, especially in Origen's case, was only of a very partial kind. He was still strongly influenced by the mathematical ideal of unity. He kept that concept of unity in his understanding of the Father, with the result that he was forced to ascribe a radically subordinate position to the Son within the godhead. This side of his thought could (and did) lead to Arianism. But it was clearly a sub-ordinate position within the godhead, and there-fore also a differentiation within the godhead, of which he was speaking. And that side of his thought could (and did) contribute to the theology of the Cappadocians. With them the repudiation of a mathematical conception of unity is a con-tinually recurring refrain. The unity of *ousia* (though certainly for them, as we have argued earlier, a real and not just a conceptual unity) is not to be identified with the bare one of arithmetical enumeration.[1] Thus, whatever the inherent diffi-culties of the Cappadocian teaching, it can properly be said that they were attempting to incorporate the new ideas of the full and substantial divinity of the Son and of the Spirit into the old pattern of monotheistic faith by a modification of the idea of unity as previously understood.

Alongside this comparatively familiar story, we may set another example of development in which can be seen a failure to make the same kind of modification. The doctrine of the unity of the Church is grounded in the fact of the unity of God. The link between the two is fundamental to the thought of Ignatius. His call for a unity of believers, centred upon the person of the bishop, reads in places as if it were no more than practical

[1] Basil, *De Spir. San.* 44–5; Greg. Naz. *Or.* 29. 2; 31. 31; Basil (really Evagrius), *Ep.* 8. 2.

advice in the face of the danger of heresy. But behind the advice is a continually recurring insistence on the unity of God, which is its fundamental ground and justification.[1] Cyprian, in the first treatise to be written directly on the subject, uses the same imagery to describe the unity of the Church which his 'master' Tertullian had used to describe the unity of God.[2] Cyprian's understanding of that unity was of the most rigorous kind. The visible Church was the one ark of salvation. Outside it there could be no salvation. And since the sacrament of baptism was the means of entering the Church and of the reception of salvation, it followed that outside the Church there could be no baptism. In all this Cyprian was no innovator; he was simply giving more precise expression to the generally held Christian position. But the situation in Cyprian's day was changing. In earlier generations when the main rivals to the orthodox Church were Marcionite or Valentinian Gnostics, it might be possible to regard them as essentially indistinguishable from the heathen. But when you are dealing with one who is only a schismatic, fully orthodox and outstandingly pious (and Novatian, the originator of the Novatianist schism in Cyprian's own day, was almost certainly both),

[1] E.g. *Magnesians*, 7; *Philadelphians*, 8; *Smyrnaeans*, 12.
[2] Cf. Cyprian, *De Un. Cath. Eccl.* 5, and Tertullian, *Adv. Prax.* 8. The comparison is clearly set out by J. P. Brisson, *Autonomisme et Christianisme dans l'Afrique Romaine* (1958), pp. 41–2.

10-2

it is not so easy. Cyprian remained unaffected by these new facts; not so the church of Rome. We cannot be sure of all the reasons which led Stephen, the bishop of Rome, to recognize schismatic baptism. Our knowledge of him comes too largely from the pen of Cyprian, who was bitterly opposed to his policy. But there can be little doubt that his primary motives were practical and pastoral—the virtual impossibility of simply identifying the schismatic with the heathen, and the desirability of easing the path of the schismatic's entry into the Church.

For these reasons Stephen's policy gained ground in the years following his death. If it is difficult to treat a schismatic as no different from a heathen, it is still more difficult to treat a second or third generation schismatic, who has had no part in the initiation of the schism, in that light. Such was Augustine's position in relation to the Donatists living nearly a century after the origin of the schism in the days of Caecilian and Donatus. Augustine had no doubt about the rightness of Stephen's policy, which since the time of the Council of Arles in A.D. 314 had become the established practice of the Catholic church. Indeed, he extended its scope to apply not merely to schismatic baptisms but to their ordinations as well. But such a policy was patently in need of theological justification. How could such an approach to schismatic sacraments be fitted into the basic Cyprianic understanding of the unity of the Church?

This problem could have been tackled in the same kind of way as the problem of the godhead was tackled—by a modification of the concept of unity. Two ways immediately suggest themselves in which this might have been done. The first two affirmations of the creed about the Church are its unity and its holiness. At the heart of Augustine's case against the Donatists is a protest at their misunderstanding of the nature of the Church's holiness. True holiness, says Augustine, cannot be demanded as an empirical characteristic of the Church here and now; it is rather an eschatological mark of the Church that is to be. It would have been possible for Augustine to argue similarly that the true unity of the Church is eschatological rather than empirical, that it belongs to the final goal rather than to the present condition of the Church. Alternatively it would have been possible for him so to broaden the concept of the Church's unity that it would be understood not exclusively of the one organization of the Catholic church but inclusively of the schismatics as well. But although it is true that he speaks of the Donatists as rending the unity of Christ, this never amounts to a view of schism as something contained within the one Church. Cyprian had used similar language about the Novatianists, and there can be no doubt about what he meant by it.[1] Schism is still understood by Augustine as a going outside the one Church.

It is argued by Dom Butler that the method of assimilation which I am here suggesting that Augustine might have followed would cease to be a 'development of theology' and constitute a 'doctrinal revolution'.[2] But this is a highly unsatisfactory distinction to draw. The example of Copernicus is only one of many illustrations of how what appears from one approach to be a complete revolution constitutes in fact the truest expression of development. Moreover, there is an inescapable arbitrariness about the application of this distinction. Butler disallows the development of the idea of the Church here suggested, on the ground that it is a revolution involving the rejection of the Cyprianic (and general patristic) principle of the visible and indivisible nature of the Church. On the other hand, he allows his own use of the principle of 'good faith' to be a justifiable interpretation of the Cyprianic (and general patristic) principle that there is no salvation outside the Church, when it seems to me at least to be every bit as much a doctrinal revolution (albeit a very desirable one) as the reinterpretation here suggested of the idea of the unity of the Church.[3]

[1] Aug. *Ep.* XLIII. 8. 21; Cyprian, *Ep.* 46. 1. Cf. B. C. Butler, *The Idea of the Church* (1962), p. 111.
[2] *Ibid.* pp. 128, 137, 159.
[3] *Ibid.* ch. IX.

Be that as it may, Augustine emphatically does not assimilate the new insights about schismatic sacraments by any process of conscious modification of the Cyprianic doctrine of the unity of the Church. The foundation pattern of the old beliefs is left unchanged. The new attitude to schismatic sacraments had therefore to be fitted into the old pattern as best it could; it is an awkward appendage tacked on to a system of thought which it does not really fit. A distinction had to be drawn between the validity and the efficacy of a sacrament which had no other *raison d'être* than to justify the holding together of two incompatible beliefs. Certainly it was good that the new insights were not simply denied and suppressed because they could not be fitted into the old pattern. A temporary stage of theological untidiness is to be preferred to the dead hand of an unalterable system that will not admit the existence of facts which do not conform to its own restrictive canons. But it is the task of theological study to assimilate new insights as tidily as can be done without distortion. The method of assimilation used in this case of simply adding on a new, and in essence incompatible, qualification can hardly be regarded as very satisfactory.

The unsatisfactory nature of this way of assimilating new insights is more than a question of aesthetic distaste for an untidy system. When taken in conjunction with that tendency to ontologize of which we have spoken earlier, it has practical as well as theoretical disadvantages. The concept of validity of orders was developed by Augustine as a way of giving some sort of recognition to schismatics, even though in the light of his general understanding of the Church he could not conceive of them as having any spiritual efficacy. But in the course of time validity becomes thought of as something in its own right apart from the particular theological context within which and for which it was initially developed; it comes to be thought of as a peculiar quality which sacraments need to possess. As such it has ceased to be a helpful concept reaching out beyond the frontiers of a rigidly unitary conception of the Church; it has often become, instead, a barrier blocking those frontiers at the point where other pressures have already helped to break them down. Today we hear talk of sacraments enjoying spiritual efficacy but lacking the further requirement of validity. The theological concepts which Augustine devised as an appendage to explain new insights in terms of the Cyprianic doctrine of the Church have themselves become the cardinal concepts of a new pattern. In their original role they were untidy but serviceable; in their later role they are a disaster.

It is clear enough from the change of attitude towards schismatic sacraments between the time of Cyprian and the time of Augustine that the early

Church was sensitive to the pressure of experience upon the articulation of her ideas. This is an important and valuable feature in the story of doctrinal development. But my contention here has been that in assimilating the lessons of that new experience the Church did not always assimilate them in the best conceivable manner. Moreover, this failure to modify earlier convictions so as to accommodate in the most coherent way the lessons of new experience was in the long run much more than a mere weakness of systematic presentation. It could in its turn give rise to more serious misunderstandings. In some cases the early belief was in need of some fairly radical modification. If that was not made, then like an infected spring it could poison a whole stream of subsequent development. I have suggested that something of this kind has happened in the case of the idea of valid but non-efficacious sacraments. But a far clearer example, where the results are evident within the patristic age itself, is provided by the particular sacrament of baptism and the ideas of forgiveness associated with it.

In speaking of baptismal forgiveness, second-century writers regularly speak of it as retrospective in character. It is a natural enough idea. The simplest conception of baptism is as a washing, and washing suggests a getting rid of the failures of the past, a wiping clean of the slate. But baptism was also a once-for-all, unrepeatable occasion. As the early second-century writer Hermas puts it, 'there is no repentance save that which took place when we went down into the water and obtained remission of our former sins'.[1] The combination of these two ideas—the exclusively retrospective and the unrepeatable character of baptism—provided the Church with the severe pastoral problem of what was to be done in cases of serious post-baptismal sin. Hermas was aware of the problem and proposed the solution of the naive would-be reformer. God, he affirmed, was allowing one special opportunity of a second repentance for all who had fallen away since their baptism; then, with the backsliders safely gathered in, the Church could resume its old course of allowing only the one repentance when in their baptism men receive the forgiveness of their former sins. But such a solution was clearly no solution. Some more permanent way of dealing with post-baptismal sin had to be developed. Since baptism could not avail, something else must be provided in its place. So grew up the penitential system, designed not merely to test the genuineness of a man's penitence, but designed, as Tertullian puts it, to 'stand in the stead of God's indignation' and 'to discharge eternal punishments'.[2]

[1] *M.* 4. 3. 1.
[2] *De Poenitentia*, 9. It may be added as a further illustration of the complexity of the process of development that the idea of 'satisfaction' seems to have made its first appearance in this context of post-baptismal forgiveness and from there to have found its way into atonement doctrine (cf. G. Aulén, *Christus Victor* (1931), pp. 97–8).

This example that we have given is given also by Newman, in the revised version of his essay on development, as his one example of a development by logical sequence. Starting from the view that the distinguishing gift of baptism was 'the plenary forgiveness of sins past', he goes on to show the logical necessity of the subsequently developed system of pardons, penances, purgatory as a form of penance, meritorious works, and the monastic rule.[1] The logical necessity of at least the earlier part of that sequence may be freely admitted. But Newman fails to consider the possibility that what was really needed was a modification of his starting-point. The alternative (and surely preferable) solution to the question of post-baptismal forgiveness is the modification of the original conviction from which the whole development took its origin. If the distinguishing gift of baptism be regarded not as 'the plenary forgiveness of sins past' but rather as the establishment of a relationship between man and God in which sin as a barrier to that relationship is dealt with once for all, then no special problem arises. Despite the imagery of washing there is nothing which requires that the forgiveness which is conveyed in baptism should be exclusively related to sins of the past.[2]

[1] *Doctrine of Development* (1878), pp. 381 ff.
[2] For a fuller statement of the point made here, see my 'One Baptism for the Remission of Sins', *C.Q.R.* CLXV (1964), 59–66.

This illustration from the single issue of post-baptismal forgiveness shows with great clarity how far-reaching are the effects where an initial conviction, which was only partially true, has been allowed to remain unmodified by subsequent experience. Its repercussions will be felt in the whole range of interrelated doctrines associated with it. In every attempt to evaluate the developing course of Christian doctrine, we need to watch not only the logical sequence of the various stages; we need always to ask also whether some undetected error near the beginning of the road may not have set the compass off the true course. Logic will only lead in the right direction if it has started from the right point.

I have tried to show that, at least in the case of the doctrines of the Church and of baptismal forgiveness, the course of development was one that is open to serious criticism. The fundamental shortcoming was the tendency to treat earlier convictions as irrevocably fixed, the failure to modify the old pattern of belief into which new ideas were being fitted. If the same shortcoming is to be found in other aspects of doctrinal development as well, it would constitute a serious weakness of which careful account would have to be taken in any assessment of the nature of development. It is therefore worth asking whether failures of a similar kind are to be detected in the more basic doctrines of the Trinity and of Christology. It is

not an easy question to answer. I have already
argued that in the case of trinitarian doctrine there
was a fruitful modification of the concept of unity.
But it may reasonably be claimed that that modification was not radical enough. Eunomius and the
Cappadocians both started from essentially Platonist presuppositions about the nature of God and of
the world. Eunomius was the more thorough-
going and consistent of the two in the application
of those presuppositions. The Cappadocians made
a valiant attempt to modify them in a way which
would enable them to do more justice to what they
regarded as the inescapable experience of revelation. But the framework of their thought remained
stubbornly resistant to their efforts. They could not
avoid allowing some serious inconsistencies within
their systems if they were not going to deny some
vital aspect of the faith.

While the Cappadocians were doing battle with
Eunomius, another struggle was going on in the
Christological field between the Antiochenes and
Apollinarius. Nothing would have horrified Apollinarius more than to find himself classed in any
way with Eunomius. But it can be argued that
if Eunomius' system is the outcome of a
thorough-going application of a Platonic cosmology
to Christian thought about the godhead, that of
Apollinarius is, in part at least, the outcome of an
equally thorough-going application of a Platonic

anthropology to thought about the person of Christ. Here too, then, it may be said, his opponents were justified in resisting his conclusions, even though, being unable to shake themselves wholly free of that anthropology which in general outline was common to both sides, it was at the cost of having to incorporate directly paradoxical language into their own affirmations.

In neither of these two instances can it be claimed, as I believe it can be claimed in the previous instances of the Church and of baptismal forgiveness, that we have a clear case of failing to modify the old form of belief in order to incorporate new insights. The kind of modification that would have been required would have constituted a complete reorientation of men's basic ways of thinking. To suggest that it represents a failure in thought is to suggest that the Fathers should have been other people than they were or indeed could have been. Moreover, it has yet to be shown that any such reorientation of ideas as is here proposed would have led to any more satisfying result. It is by no means certain that the task is one that can be done at all. But to contemplate the possibility may perhaps provide a glimpse of how drastic and how difficult a process any fruitful development of doctrine in the future is likely to prove.

8

TOWARDS A DOCTRINE
OF DEVELOPMENT

THE great doctrinal definitions of the early Church were the outcome of a closely contested process of reasoning. My aim in this study has been to give a critical review of some of the main aspects of that reasoning process. In particular we have considered three of the fundamental grounds of argumentation: the appeals to Scripture, to the experience of worship, and to the requirements of soteriology; and two important aspects of the way in which the reasoning was conducted: the tendency to objectification and the manner of incorporating new ideas into an existing body of agreed doctrine. In the course of this survey I have suggested a number of points at which the reasoning used seems to me to be open to serious criticism. Not everyone will agree with all the points that I have made, but equally few will, I imagine, be prepared to claim that the reasoning of the Fathers in these matters is wholly free from blemish. The final question we have to raise is what conclusions ought to be drawn from such a survey about the nature of the development of doctrine and about the attitude which it is reasonable to adopt towards the conclusions reached by the early Church.

In making such an assessment we need to beware of two extreme positions. Some may be tempted to claim that reasons are not really very important, that in this case, as in many other realms of human thought, the reasons overtly given are really a blind, a rationalization of judgements actually based upon quite other grounds. It is undoubtedly true that men are often moved by hidden motives which not even they themselves fully understand. I do not believe that it follows from this fact that the process of argumentation in such cases is necessarily reduced to a façade of no significance in itself. The objection would have more force in this instance if the kind of reasoning employed by the Fathers were of a purely formal or historical kind. In that event it would be difficult to account for the depth of passion which was felt on both sides. But this is not the case; the reasoning used was of a much broader kind. Scripture, it is true, was sometimes treated as a set of propositional statements from which the truth could be read off by a process of deductive logic. But Scripture was never the sole court of appeal. The living tradition of the Church included not only the historical facts recorded in Scripture but also the continuing and contemporary experience of Christians. The reality of worship and of salvation were issues in which men's deepest feelings and aspirations were involved. These were recognized and expressed in the arguments that were employed. The kind of reasons to which the Fathers appealed were reasons which did justice to the fact that the determination of religious issues is not a matter in which the intellect alone is involved, but one in which man's experience of worship and of the moral life also has to be taken into account.

But if there is a danger of underestimating the importance of the reasons used in reaching doctrinal decisions, there is also a danger of overestimating it. We must not assume that if the chain of reasoning used can be shown to be invalid in some respect, the whole structure must necessarily collapse. Any valid criticism of the arguments used is a serious challenge to the system of beliefs which was established with the aid of those arguments; but it is not its automatic demolition. The unarticulated apprehension of a truth may sometimes be surer than the reasons which are subsequently produced in justification of it.[1] It is not an uncommon occurrence in philosophy for an argument to be shown to have a less coercive force than it was believed to possess when first developed, but for its conclusion to remain unshaken and for the

[1] Cf. K. Rahner, 'The Development of Dogma', in *Theological Investigations*, I, 55.

argument itself to continue to be of importance when revised and re-expressed in less precise or deductive form. The traditional arguments for the existence of God could be quoted in illustration. Many of those who would be most ready to point to fallacies in their traditional and strict form of expression would still wish to assert that in suitably revised form they remain significant pointers to that reality of God which they were designed to establish. Even if the reasoning of the Fathers be judged to have serious weaknesses in the form in which it was first put forward, we must not conclude too hastily that it is altogether worthless and its conclusions completely discredited.

In the light of these general considerations we may look in more detail at the central Christian doctrine of the divinity of Christ. The three great grounds of appeal, Scripture, worship and soteriology, all contributed to the affirmation of the doctrine, and we must begin by summarizing briefly in the light of our earlier studies the contribution of each of these grounds to the determination of the doctrine.

The outstanding characteristic of the witness of Scripture in the matter is its ambiguity. Once the doctrine of the full divinity of Christ was put forward, there was plenty of evidence that could very reasonably be used in its support. How else could one account for such words as 'I and my

Father are one' (John x. 30)? But there was also plenty of evidence that seemed to tell against it. Jesus also said 'Why callest thou me good? There is none good but one, that is God' (Mark x. 18). The Fathers were conscious that there were such apparent difficulties. They believed that they could overcome them, but they only did so by means of a method of exegesis which few today would feel able to accept. In addition it has to be said that much of the evidence which the Fathers sincerely believed to be in full support of their doctrine did not really support it as directly as they thought. They believed that when St Paul spoke of Christ Jesus as 'being in the form of God' (Phil. ii. 6) he meant the same as they meant when they spoke of the Son as being *homoousios* with the Father. In this, in at any rate the most straightforward sense of the word 'meaning', they were certainly wrong. This does not mean that the *homoousios* doctrine is a totally illegitimate interpretation of Paul's teaching. But it must at least be allowed to suggest that, in terms of the interpretation of the scriptural text alone, it may not be as exclusive or as necessary an interpretation as has often been claimed. The appeal to Scripture cannot be dismissed as wholly invalid. But neither is it as clear or as unambiguous as the Fathers believed it to be. If the doctrine is to be accepted as true, it needs other support. How far do the other two grounds of patristic appeal supply the measure of support that is needed?

The second ground of appeal to be considered is that of worship. . We have seen the important role which this factor played from a very early stage. Christ was worshipped by people who were genuinely shocked at any suggestion that they could even contemplate worshipping a fellow human being. Even the angels were no more than fellow servants; only God was to be worshipped (cf. Rev. xxii. 8–9). Here again we have an argument which is not without force but which, when examined critically, does not have quite such compelling force as it might seem at first sight to possess. At the point where the worship of Christ was of decisive significance for the development of doctrine, it was a question of popular devotion rather than formal liturgical worship. Popular devotion is not without significance but it is no infallible guide. Its history is full of examples of confusion between the medium and the ultimate object of worship, between the image and the reality. It is not clear that we are in a position to rule out the possibility of something of the same kind having happened in this case also.

The third ground of appeal is the one that has frequently been regarded as the most important of all. The Christian message of salvation, it is claimed, would cease to exist without a clear insistence on the unqualified divinity of Christ. I have already argued at some length that this claim does not seem to me to be as compelling as it has normally been asserted to be.[1] The argument from soteriology can be analysed as having three possible aspects. It could take the form of an argument that God *must* have acted in a particular way in order to meet man's need, quite apart from any reference to how he has actually acted in history. It is difficult to see how any such natural knowledge of divine necessity could seriously be affirmed. It may, secondly, be based on the evidence of how God has actually revealed that he does save in the historic saving acts of Christ. In that way it would be simply a special case of the appeal to Scripture which we have already considered. In the third place, it could take the form of an appeal to the present experience of salvation.[2] The fact that that experience is so intimately bound up with the facts of Christ's life, death and resurrection and the way in which the fruit of that work is experienced as a living reality through the power of the Spirit might be decisive evidence that it is in and through Christ that God has acted for the salvation of men. It is not easy to see how our present experience could be decisive evidence for

[1] See pp. 106–13 above.

[2] On the important role of this kind of appeal, see D. E. Nineham, 'Some Reflections on the Present Position with regard to the Jesus of History', *C.Q.R.* CLXVI (1965), 12–13.

the precise nature and manner of God's active presence in Jesus.

Thus the main lines of patristic argument for the divinity of Jesus are not worthless, but they do not seem to me to be decisive either. That is not by any means to say that the main alternative of the patristic age, namely Arianism, is to be preferred. Similar difficulties, difficulties indeed of a far greater order of magnitude, could be raised in the case of Arianism also. It is rather to say that the terms in which the patristic age posed the question were not terms in which it could be satisfactorily settled.

Some will be tempted to conclude from that admission that Gibbon was right after all, that there was nothing more to Nicaea than the addition or omission of one iota, that the doctrinal history of the early Church is a tale told by a host of idiots, full of sound and fury, signifying nothing. But the temptation is one to which it would be wrong to succumb. The history of science shows many instances of generations struggling with issues for which they had not got the necessary equipment to produce a satisfactory settlement. Such struggles do inevitably involve a good deal of wasted labour, but they are not just a sheer waste of time. Such a struggle does not normally result in mere frustration. It may not be able to solve the precise problem which it set out to solve, but it is not normally unproductive. Out of the struggle a fruitful way of advance emerges, even though it may be along very different lines than had been originally expected.

We must at all costs refuse to accept the dilemma that the doctrinal decisions of the early Church were either valueless or totally free from error. In general terms we may claim that they served the Church well and yet insist that they were marked at every point by the imperfection of her members and the shortcomings of their reasoning. A judgement of this kind is so vague as to be virtually without value in itself. It is no more than a rough delineation of the area within which the answer to our fundamental quest is to be sought. We have to go on and ask whether it is possible to delineate with any more precision the nature of this valuable, yet eminently fallible, development of doctrine that has taken place.

'Development of doctrine' is an impressive phrase, but without further definition it lacks content. The idea of radical discontinuity in doctrine is not strictly conceivable. There must always be a relation of some sort between what has gone before and what comes after. Nicene orthodoxy can clearly and properly be presented as a development of earlier beliefs. But, if Arianism had prevailed, the same could quite legitimately have been said about it also. And that would apply to any other historically conceivable alternative definition of the faith that might have been accepted, for it would not be historically conceivable unless it stood in some kind of continuity with what had gone before. Even revolutions have their germinating seeds within the pre-revolutionary situation. It is never enough, therefore, to show that later doctrine is a development of earlier. Our search is for criteria which will enable us to say why one development is true and another false, or even why one development is in some respects truer than another. In the case of Nicene orthodoxy it is tempting to suggest that it was the true development because it gave the 'highest' account of the person of Christ, because it took most seriously the worshipping tradition of the Church. But such a criterion is clearly unreliable. It was just such an approach which was responsible for the conviction of Eutyches and the Monophysites that their teaching must be the true expression of the faith. We need to look for criteria of a more general kind, and we can best begin by a closer analysis of the concept of development itself.

Many analogies have been used at different times in attempts to throw light on the nature of development. These have been drawn particularly from the realm of the natural sciences. Evolution and the growth of an organism have offered useful analogies. But the most valuable parallels are provided not so much by objects within the natural world as by other examples of development in the realm of human thought. Every field of human thought has a history. That history always includes development in some sense, though the degree to which it is a record of progressive development varies considerably. The history of science appears at first sight to be a very straightforward case of progressive development. The story is a less straightforward one than it appears initially to be, but the genuinely progressive character of the development is beyond dispute. At the other extreme the history of art or of philosophy reads more like a series of variations on a theme, in which progressive development, even though it may be present in some degree, is certainly not a dominant factor. Other subjects, such as development in historical method, stand somewhere between these two extremes.

Theology has important points of contact with all these widely differing spheres of human thought. Its ways of working are not simply to be identified with any one of them. But we may well hope to deepen our understanding of the nature of doctrinal development by comparison with the pattern of development in those fields like science and historiography where its working is most clearly to be seen.

The phrase 'Copernican revolution' is in danger of becoming a cliché to describe any major change in the realm of ideas. This must not be allowed to destroy its importance as the most striking illustration of the way in which some of the most important developments in human thought have come about. The nature of the scientific revolution was enormously complex; in some respects it can be made to appear very gradual, in others remarkably abrupt. The new ways grew out of the old. The old system had not died; it had not been abandoned, leaving a vacuum which something had to fill. Up to a point the old system still worked very well. It was not so decadent or unserviceable that only an incorrigible traditionalist could continue to support it. Some problems it did not solve satisfactorily at all; others it solved only in a very clumsy and complicated fashion. But the new way did not solve all these outstanding difficulties overnight. In some cases it clearly did better; had it not done so it would hardly have been proposed by intelligent scholars. But in other respects it showed no improvement at all at the start. Indeed, for some practical purposes, like navigation and surveying, the Ptolemaic system is still generally employed.[1] The determinative factor in ensuring the triumph of the new ideas was not so much their tidying up of the thought of the past as their creativeness in

[1] Cf. T. S. Kuhn, *The Copernican Revolution* (1957), p. 37. The work of T. S. Kuhn, particularly his book *The Structure of Scientific Revolutions* (1963), is most illuminating on this whole question.

relation to the future. It was the way in which they opened up new possibilities of advance that finally won the day. These further advances were only made possible once the new ideas had been allowed effectively to replace the old, even though the old had still much to be said on their behalf.

The moral of the story would seem to be that the way of creative development in the scientific field must involve a readiness to 'forget those things which are behind and reach out to those things which are before' (cf. Phil. iii. 13). The test of a possible new development must never be how much of the old can be retained in its old form. It may be at this point that the Church has most to learn about the proper course for doctrinal development. The Church as an institution is of a naturally conservative temper. In practice she seems frequently to have regarded the true development as that which involved the least measure of negation of past doctrinal formulation.[1] But this is a most unsatisfactory test. As with later refinements of the Ptolemaic system, it leads to very clumsy and complicated solutions of some problems. More seriously still, it may preclude the effective raising of other new but vitally important problems altogether.

If the continuity in the development of doctrine is not to be seen in a set of unchanging and

[1] See chapter 7 above.

unchangeable dogmas, where is it to be located? A partial answer, at least, might be that it is to be seen in a continuity of fundamental aims. An answer of this kind has been proposed in the course of recent discussion in the Roman Catholic church. Bishop de Smedt has argued that in the last century the Church condemned religious liberty when it was proposed by men who had a rationalistic misconception of the jurisdictional omnipotence of the state and who regarded the individual conscience as subject to no law or divinely given norm; now, so he claims, the ideal of religious liberty has been severed from that political context and the Church is ready to proclaim that it is a natural right of man—all in the interest of the one cause of human freedom. Father Baum, who quotes this example, sees a similar possibility of development in the Church's attitude to contraception. Here, he suggests, a radical change in the Church's actual attitude could still be expressive of a continuity in concern for the fruitfulness of married life within a new setting of sociological conditions and anthropological knowledge.[1] In both these cases the element of sheer error in the earlier judgements of the Church seems to have been unjustifiably played down. But that point need not concern us here. The kind of development which is postulated in each case is surely the

[1] Ed. T. D. Roberts, *Contraception and Holiness* (1964), pp. 277–80.

kind for which we should be looking. The continuity is seen in the continuity of aim and objective.

The same principle can be applied to the sphere of those basic Christian doctrines with which this study has been primarily concerned. True continuity with the age of the Fathers is to be sought not so much in the repetition of their doctrinal conclusions or even in the building upon them, but rather in the continuation of their doctrinal aims. Their doctrinal affirmations were based upon an appeal to the record of Scripture, the activity of worship, and the experience of salvation. Should not true development be seen in the continuation of the attempt to do justice to those three strands of Christian life in the contemporary world? If we accept that development is to be understood in such terms, we cannot rule out in advance the possibility that it could involve shifts in doctrinal affirmation as radical as those embodied for science in the Copernican revolution or reversals of judgement as drastic as those envisaged in the case of religious liberty or (hypothetically) of contraception. Father Baum quotes contemporary concern, both Christian and secular, with the question Who is man? as the basis of a changed outlook on sexuality calling for a new development in teaching about contraception. Such changes in the understanding of human nature, vividly illustrated but not exclusively delineated by the teaching of Freud, have their relevance for every sphere of Christian doctrine.

The idea of a doctrinal revolution is therefore not something of which we have cause to be afraid. Indeed, in view of all the contemporary changes in man's understanding of himself and his world, it is something to be expected. Judging from the analogy of the history of science, it need not prove as totally destructive of past ideas as it is likely at first to appear to be. It may be the only, even though painful, path to constructive advance. If we speak in such terms of an incipient doctrinal revolution, we must never make the mistake of imagining that we are about to usher in the eschatological age in theology. Newtonian physics was a revolutionary development in its own day, but in due course it had to yield to that of Einstein. Revolutions of this kind are not eschatological events; they are part of a continuing process of development. But with that warning we may usefully go on to ask whether there are any indications of the direction in which the development of doctrine—be that development revolutionary in character or not—might most fruitfully move.

One aspect of early doctrinal development which stood out in our survey was the tendency to objectification. This, I suggested, can be seen as the source of a number of the problems and difficulties which we feel today about early doctrinal formulations.[1] Such objectification is proving itself today to be an unworkable concept even in those spheres, like theoretical physics, where it seemed most clearly applicable. Even in such fields the role played by the human observer is being found to be something which cannot be ignored or eliminated. Christians have often been afraid that any shift away from the objectivity of traditional doctrinal thinking will open the sluice-gates to an unqualified subjectivity. Some recent attempts to theologize in this manner show that such fears are not without foundation. But thought, like life, is never free from risk. We are not, however, faced with a choice between two complete opposites. Modern developments in historiography may provide a useful illustration. Few would now wish to claim that a completely neutral and therefore definitive history, such as that to which Lord Acton aspired, is possible.[2] There are no bare historical facts of the kind which such a theory assumes; or, at least, in so far as there are such facts their simple recitation does not constitute the writing of history. The writing of history involves a degree of interpretation which depends in some measure upon the personal standpoint of the historian and the problems of his age. But this does not reduce the writing of history to the writing

[1] See chapter 6 above.
[2] Cf. Sir George Clark, *New Cambridge Modern History*, General Introduction, pp. xxiv–xxv.

of rival forms of propaganda; it does not destroy the real measure of impartiality or objectivity in critical or 'scientific' historical research. This remains an indispensable element in historical work; but so is the interpretative role of the historian himself. The position of the theologian is not dissimilar. If he should find himself unable any longer to speak about God in himself, God apart from our experience of him, in the fully objective way that the majority of his predecessors have done, he would not thereby be reduced to talking in a purely subjective way about his own experiences. The fact that it may never be possible to remove the *quoad nos* from any statement about God does not mean that we are unable to speak in any real sense about God at all. To abandon talk about God in himself is not to abandon talk about God altogether; nor is it to imply that he only exists for our sake, for the meeting of our human needs.

It may be that there is a pointer here to the kind of direction that doctrinal development might take. To abandon all talk about the one *ousia* and the three *hupostaseis* of the godhead would certainly be a revolutionary development away from traditional doctrinal formulations. Yet the seeds of that revolution are present in the very writers who were responsible for the initial development of the traditional language. The Cappadocians frequently stress that the divine *ousia* is both inaccessible and unknowable. It is the divine activity (ἐνέργεια) which alone impinges directly upon mankind. Even the term godhead (θεότης) was for them expressive of the divine activity rather than the divine nature.[1] But their great opponent Eunomius was prepared to speak of a unity of Father and Son in respect of the divine activity and at the same time to assert a full knowledge of the divine *ousia* on the basis of which Father and Son were to be described as totally different at that level.[2] The most obvious counter to such teaching was to affirm an identity of *ousia* as the Cappadocians did. But if it once be admitted that we cannot speak meaningfully in this way of the divine *ousia* in itself, then the ground is cut from under Eunomius' feet. If such an approach makes it impossible to draw the same distinctions in belief which the Fathers drew, to tell, for example, whether a man is a Sabellian or not, this is not necessarily the disaster which Dr Mascall believes it to be.[3] The test of a true development in doctrine is not whether it preserves all the distinctions of the old in their old form; it is whether it continues the objectives of the Church in her earlier doctrinal work in a way which is effective and creative in the contemporary world.

[1] Basil, *Ep.* 234, 1; Greg. Nyss. *Con. Eun.* (ed. Jaeger), II, 106-7, 148-50; *On Not Three Gods* (ed. Jaeger), III, i. 44-5. Cf. also Chrys. *Hom. in Joh.* 2. 4 (*P.G.* 59, 34).
[2] Eunomius, *Apology*, 23-4.
[3] *Up and Down in Adria*, p. 71, in criticism of the essay in *Sounding* by H. W. Montefiore, 'Towards a Christology for Today'.

A similar approach is clearly possible in the realm of Christology also. Eucharistic theology grew up in the shadow of Christological doctrine. The combination of the two realities, earthly and heavenly, in the eucharistic body of Christ was very properly understood to be derivative from the prior union of the two natures in the incarnate Christ himself. A good many today would feel that a more satisfactory eucharistic theology would be one which stressed the divine-human nature of the whole eucharistic action rather than one which spoke of the co-presence of two objectively existing realities in the eucharistic elements. Might not a similar development be appropriate to the prototype also, to the doctrine of the person of Christ himself?

An attempt to show the form which such a development might take has been made by H. W. Montefiore in his essay in *Soundings*. It cannot, I think, be denied that such an undertaking stands fully in line with those three objectives which we have defined as constituting the essence of the doctrinal task, the aim to do justice to the witness of Scripture, of worship, and of salvation. Montefiore himself quotes Dix and Cullmann as stressing the way in which the primary concern of the New Testament is with the function of Christ rather than with his nature.[1] Such quotations could be multiplied many times over. It is perhaps worth

[1] *Soundings*, p. 159.

emphasizing that this priority of concern characterizes not only the New Testament writings in
general but also the incipient forms of credal
confession to be found there. E. Schweizer writes
in an essay entitled 'Two New Testament Creeds
compared: I Cor. 15.3–5 and I Tim. 3.16': 'The
content of both creeds is God's deed in Jesus
Christ... This is the unity of both creeds and
it is true, more or less, for all other ancient strata
of credal statements in the New Testament.'[1] It
should not be suggested, as Montefiore fully
recognizes, that such an approach to Christology
in terms of the divine activity therefore represents
a return from the false accretions of patristic and
scholastic teaching to the one true and biblical
form of Christological doctrine. But it is clear
evidence that such an approach is fully in accord
with the first basis of doctrinal work, faithfulness
to the witness of Scripture. The same can be said
also of the other two basic grounds of doctrinal
appeal. The fundamental language of salvation is
of a work of God effected in Christ. The fundamental language of worship is of man's self-offering
to God through Christ. In both cases the language
of the divine activity seems fully as appropriate as
the traditional language of the divine being. The
detailed elaboration of such a development in

[1] Eds. W. Klassen and G. F. Snyder, *Current Issues in New Testament
Interpretation* (1962), p. 171.

doctrine will be a task of great complexity and this is not the place to attempt it. My aim is simply to suggest what might prove a proper and appropriate line for such development to take.

Two final questions remain to be asked. Granted that such an approach to doctrine would be permissible, is there any reason to believe that it would prove a productive one? It would be quite false to suggest that it would offer an easy solution to contemporary difficulties in affirming the existence of God or that it would have an immediate evangelistic appeal for those who are unimpressed by traditional orthodoxy. As with Copernicus, the creative potential of a new way of thought is not often immediately apparent. Its proponent has to depend in part upon intuition; he has to back a hunch which only the progress of time can substantiate. What I believe can be said is this. In the first place, it is an approach which seems to be capable of doing justice to the permanent aims of Christian doctrine in a way which is most naturally congruent with the pattern of human knowledge as a whole in our day. In the second place (and this is the hunch), it may prove able to do so in a way which will throw new light on what is really involved in response and obedience to God. But whether any apparently new approach really bears within itself the seeds of such creative possibilities or whether it is a purely passing fashion which will be totally counteracted in a few years by an opposing swing of the pendulum, or whether it stands somewhere between those two—that is something which only the most gifted prophet could foretell.

The second question is how we can know whether such an approach, as we try to work it out in detail, is in fact doing justice to the permanent aims of Christian doctrine. If our Christology is expressed in wholly different categories from the two-nature categories of Chalcedon, how can we know whether or not it is a true development of the earlier doctrinal formula? In the stricter sense of the word 'know' we cannot; in the nature of the case there cannot be any infallible criteria. I believe that we are more likely to prove loyal to the past, in the important sense of the word 'loyal', if we think not so much in terms of the translation of old formulae into new sets of words as in terms of the continuation of the same task of interpreting the Church's Scriptures, her worship and her experience of salvation. In our attempts to pursue that task we may still go badly astray. But it is only as the Church as a whole gives herself with full seriousness to the task that true development becomes a genuine possibility. And the only test of whether the development in question is a true one is for the Church to ask herself repeatedly whether she is expressing as fully as she is able the things to which her Scriptures, her worship and her experience of salvation bear witness.

INDEX

INDEX

INDEX